THE LEADERSHIP PARADOX

TOLERANCE AND PRIDE

DIGVIJAY MOURYA

Made with ♥ on the Notion Press Platform
www.notionpress.com

Contents

Dedication

This book is dedicated to all the leaders and sales professionals who have the courage and determination to pursue their dreams and achieve their goals.Your hard work, passion, and commitment to excellence is an inspiration to me.

I would also like to dedicate this book to my family, loved ones and my office colleague, my Directors Mr. Deepak Verma & Mr. Praveen Verma, who have supported me throughout my journey. Your unwavering love, encouragement, and understanding have been instrumental in my success, and I am grateful for your constant support and belief in me.

Finally, I dedicate this book to all the readers, who have chosen to invest their time and energy in learning and growing. I hope that this book will provide you with the knowledge,skills,and inspiration you need to succeed in leadership and sales, and that it will help you achieve your own version of success.

Thank you for joining me on this journey, and I wish you all the best in your pursuit of excellence.

Preface

Welcome, dear reader, to The Leadership Paradox by Digvijay Mourya. This book invites you to embark on an enlightening journey through the intricate dynamics of leadership—a realm where the interplay of tolerance and pride shapes the essence of effective guidance.

In our contemporary society, leadership is often idealized, presenting a façade of unwavering confidence and infallibility. Yet, beneath this veneer lies a complex tapestry woven with contradictions, challenges, and the very human experiences that define effective leaders. Through this exploration, we will unravel the myths surrounding the ideal leader and confront the harsh realities that many face in their pursuit of excellence.

This work is not merely a theoretical treatise; it is a call to action. Each chapter offers insights, real-life narratives, and actionable strategies designed to help you navigate the paradoxes that accompany leadership. You will encounter stories of leaders who have transformed their organizations through openness, vulnerability, and a commitment to fostering constructive conflict. These narratives serve as powerful reminders that embracing imperfections, fostering dialogue, and prioritizing collective growth are essential for sustainable change.

As we delve into diverse themes—from the dangers of complacency to the empowering nature of constructive conflict—remember that leadership is not a solitary endeavor. It is a shared journey where relationships, accountability, and continuous self-reflection create the foundation for growth. You will be challenged to reflect on your leadership philosophy, engage with your teams authentically, and cultivate an environment that celebrates both pride in progress and humility in learning.

As you turn the pages, I encourage you to embrace the lessons, insights, and stories that resonate with your own experiences. Let this book ignite your curiosity, inspire conversations, and ultimately guide you toward becoming the leader you aspire to be.

Thank you for joining me on this exploration of leadership's complexities. Together, let us navigate the labyrinth of human interactions, fostering a culture where vulnerability is seen as strength and where the potential for collective triumph is boundless.

Digvijay Mourya

Hey Awesome Reader!

Welcome aboard this thrilling ride through the pages of 'Enigma in the Shadows'! Buckle up, because we're about to dive into a labyrinth of suspense, mystery, and emotion that has occupied my mind for far too long. The creation of this book wasn't just a stroll through the park; it was a wild exploration of the human psyche and the shadows that dance behind our every thought. As I scribbled down my ideas, I found myself tumbling down rabbit holes of research and introspection, uncovering layers I didn't know existed. It all started with an intriguing question: what secrets lurk in the corners of our lives that we dare not confront? This question became the heartbeat of my writing process, pushing me to dig deeper into themes of fear, resilience, and redemption. Each chapter is crafted like a puzzle piece meant to connect and create a bigger picture, much like life itself. I poured my sweat, tears, and caffeine into writing this book because I believe in the power of stories to transform and transport us. You'll witness characters who are flawed yet relatable, entangled in dilemmas that mirror our own. As I wove their tales, I wanted to create a canvas bursting with colors of emotions that challenge and inspire. Research has been my loyal companion, guiding me through the murky waters of psychological exploration. I dove into studies, interviews, and anything I could consume to equip myself with knowledge to honor the complexity of the human experience. Trust me, you'll feel my fervor through every word as I meticulously crafted scenes that I hope will linger long after you've turned the final page. This book is not just meant to be read; it's an experience intended to resonate and provoke thoughts about what it means to live authentically. I want you to feel every heartbeat and pulse of tension as you navigate the journey alongside my characters. It's my hope that the themes resonate with you, sparking curiosity and discussions long after you've finished reading. Really, I poured my soul into this so that you could enjoy an adventure that's filled with twists and turns. Your engagement matters to me because it means we're connecting through this shared experience. I imagine you laughing, gasping, and possibly shedding a tear or two as you immerse yourself in this atmospheric world I've created. Each moment matters, and I challenge you to savor it all. The stories within these pages reflect bits of me but also bits of you, your experiences, and your emotions. That's the beauty of storytelling—it binds us. I'm thrilled that you've chosen this book; I can't wait for you to uncover the secrets hiding in the shadows. So grab your blanket, get cozy, and let's unravel the tapestry of 'Enigma in the Shadows' together! Here's to the journey ahead—let it grip you, challenge you, and ultimately inspire you until you reach the very last line. Enjoy every moment! It's time to turn the page!

With excitement and anticipation
Digvijay Mourya

CHAPTER ONE

THE MYTH OF IDEAL LEADERSHIP

Unpacking the Ideal Leader

In contemporary society, the concept of leadership is often romanticized. When we think of leaders, we conjure images of charismatic individuals clad in confident attire, effortlessly guiding their teams through challenges and towards success. They are decisive, fearless, and above all, revered figures. Yet, when we strip away this veneer, a complex reality unfolds, revealing numerous contradictions and challenges inherent in leadership.

Decisiveness is often heralded as a hallmark of effective leadership. Leaders are expected to analyze myriad factors and make tough decisions, often under immense pressure. Historical figures like Winston Churchill and modern-day CEOs like Indra Nooyi exemplify this trait. Churchill's resolve during World War II inspired a nation, while Nooyi's strategic decisions propelled PepsiCo into new markets. Their steadfastness instills confidence among followers, fostering a sense of assurance that they are led by individuals capable of making pivotal choices.

Yet, the very decisiveness that makes leaders admirable can also shroud them in skepticism. The pressure to appear unwavering can lead leaders to make impulsive decisions without thoroughly weighing all consequences. Churchill, while celebrated for his defiance, also made choices that incurred heavy losses, decisions that are more critically examined in academic circles today than at the time. In contrast, less flamboyant leaders, who may exhibit thoughtfulness and deliberation, can be overlooked or even criticized for their perceived indecisiveness.

Linked closely to decisiveness is the trait of confidence. Confidence exudes strength, creating an aura that persuades followers to trust a leader's vision. Individuals like Steve Jobs, known for their bold proclamations and strong belief in their products, often spurred teams to innovate, venture into uncharted territories, and redefine markets. However, confidence, when exaggerated, can morph into hubris, ultimately leading to collective downfall. Jobs' unyielding conviction often led Apple to tremendous successes, but it also caused friction and, at times, alienation within his own ranks as he dismissed alternative ideas and critical feedback.

The envy of confident leadership leads many to confuse arrogance with confidence. Leaders who proclaim their authority and disregard opposition risk alienating their teams, driving wedges that turn collaboration into strife. Take Elizabeth Holmes, the founder of Theranos, who personified confidence but ultimately misled investors and employees regarding her company's technology. Her overestimation of her capabilities and vehement rejection of dissenting opinions ultimately revealed the dangers of misplaced confidence. Such tales illustrate how confidence can seduce but also create disastrous outcomes when unchecked by humility or reflection.

Charisma, frequently touted as an essential trait of effective leaders, encapsulates the ability to draw others in. Charismatic leaders inspire followings that may deploy armies into battle, create revolutionary movements, or even launch technological advancements that change the world. Figures like Martin Luther King Jr. and Barack Obama wielded charisma that moved masses, creating momentum toward significant social and political change. Their words inspired, uplifted, and created sense of purpose among their followers.

Nevertheless, charisma carries its burdens. Historical examination often highlights leaders such as Jim Jones or Adolf Hitler, whose magnetic personalities concealed sinister motives, leading to dire consequences. Charisma enables leaders to manipulate perceptions, drawing others into a sense of loyalty that can obscure the leader's moral compass or intentions. The challenge lies in differentiating between a leader's genuine intent and manipulative rhetoric designed to fuel a personal agenda.

The confluence of decisiveness, confidence, and charisma presents a mosaic often viewed through a highly favorable lens. However, underneath these attributes, societal expectations impose unrealistic standards. The media, in its celebration of success, paints a portrait of the ideal leader that seldom reflects the authentic narratives of struggles, failures, and learning. Every leader faces moments of self-doubt, navigates conflicts, and grapples with the repercussions of their decisions. When comparisons arise between the public spectacle of leadership and the intricate web of vulnerabilities faced by everyday leaders, cognitive dissonance ensues.

Public perception is molded by societal narratives that romanticize achievements, glossing over the complexities surrounding leader decision-making. The stories we tell about leaders reinforce a singular idea that greatness comes with ease. And when real-life leaders falter or display vulnerability, society can be unforgiving. The backlash against any visible sign of struggle reiterates the perception that leaders must always embody certainty and strength, stifling the authentic experiences that can foster growth and connection.

As we explore the attributes of leaders like Angela Merkel, the former Chancellor of Germany, it is clear that perceptions surrounding leadership do not come solely from their decision-making prowess or confidence. Rather, it comes from the societal context that bears down upon them. Merkel's tenure was often characterized by resilience and pragmatism, yet she faced heavy scrutiny for her differentiation from the idealized version of a political leader. Despite her substantive achievements on issues from the Eurozone crisis to immigration, her understated demeanor made her less appealing in the eyes of some who preferred the more ostentatious styles of global counterparts.

This inconsistency creates a paradox: leaders who strive for authenticity may inadvertently be vilified for their humanity, while those who fit the mold may be celebrated despite their moral failings. The narratives surrounding ideal leadership thus often create a divide between public admiration and the real struggles leaders face.

Society's drive for idealized leadership epitomizes the fundamental flaws in our perception of success and excellence. Leaders are increasingly expected to project an image of infallibility and competence, leading to a culture that shuns vulnerability while fetishizing unyielding strength. The dichotomy of how leaders are viewed creates a powerful dichotomy, as their struggles worsen the negativity foisted upon them by those who hold them to unrealistic standards. This fosters an environment where leaders often feel compelled to uphold appearances rather than seeking help, further isolating them in their struggles.

Moreover, the disconnect between the public narrative and the realities leaders endure can breed disillusionment and fatigue. When leaders of corporations or countries feel the need to mask their doubts and reveal only their successes, it reinforces the sense of inadequacy in those who aspire to leadership while suffering in silence. The resulting pressure contributes to a cycle where real growth and learning are stifled by the demand for perfection. When the struggles of leadership are hidden, those who may benefit from witnessing authentic vulnerability will never have the opportunity to learn from these experiences.

Consequently, unpacking the ideal leader requires a meticulous exploration of the interplay between societal expectations and individual struggles. Leaders who navigate these expectations authentically can foster essential lessons about resilience, adaptability, and transparency, thus normalizing the challenges inherent in leadership roles. This endeavor demands courage and a willingness to restructure our understanding of effective leadership, harrowing as that may be.

Leaders should strive to convey their genuine narratives while creating spaces for their teams to engage authentically. This pursuit unearths not just triumphs but also setbacks that enable growth. When leaders bring their challenges into light, they foster a culture of shared experiences and communal accountability.

In our exploration of leadership, it becomes clear that no single narrative holds absolute truth. Leadership is not an isolated endeavor; instead, it sits at the intersection of individual struggles, societal expectations, and broader cultural narratives. We must encourage a conscious effort to shift the focus from the ideal leader - that fictional archetype - to the labyrinth of real human experiences that define effective leadership in practice.

As we begin to accept the imperfection of leaders, we pave the way for a movement toward more inclusive, collaborative environments. Societies that allow for nuance within the narratives of leaders can create transformative avenues for people at all organizational levels. We begin to normalize the challenges of leadership, diminish the stigma surrounding vulnerability, and create a more significant understanding of the complexities that govern human interactions.

By reconstructing our expectations of leaders and acknowledging their narratives, we can transform our perception of leadership from one rigidly committed to unattainable standards toward a dynamic framework that champions growth, humility, and resilience. The story of leadership is as multifaceted as the characters we place as leaders, illuminating the paths many forge through uncertainty and complexity. We must reject the myth of the ideal leader while embracing the reality of shared experiences and collective triumphs, thereby redefining leadership for generations to come.

The Shadow of Perfection

In the pursuit of ideal leadership, many find themselves chasing a mirage: perfection. The societal pressures and ingrained beliefs surrounding what a leader should embody often create an oppressive atmosphere where flaws are forbidden. This chapter explores the detrimental effects of perfectionism in leadership, offering real-world case studies of leaders who, in striving for an unattainable ideal, faced severe consequences both personally and professionally. Through their narratives, we will uncover the burdens of perfectionism and the invaluable lessons learned when they began to embrace their own imperfections.

The Illusion of Perfection

For many leaders, the notion of perfectionism manifests as a relentless quest. They equate leadership with a flawless execution of vision, expecting themselves to always deliver results without error. This mindset, while well-intentioned, can easily morph into an obsession that clouds judgment and inhibits genuine connection with team members. The fear of making mistakes often leads to an inability to take calculated risks, stifling creativity and innovation.

Dr. Melissa Carr, a former CEO at a tech startup, encapsulates the peril of this mindset. "I thought being perfect would earn me respect and trust. Instead, it turned my team into robots—overly cautious and fearful of making mistakes," she shares in a candid interview. Melissa's initial years as a leader were consumed by the desire to present a polished image both internally and externally. However, the pressure took a toll both on her mental health and the morale of her team.

As she pushed her team towards an impossible standard, she inadvertently fostered an environment where vulnerability was shunned. "I remember holding meetings where I would demand 'perfection' in each project. My team became so terrified of disappointing me that they'd rather stay silent than voice a creative idea or admit a shortcoming," Melissa recalls. The repercussions of her perfectionism resulted in stagnation, poor morale, and eventually, turnover.

The Breaking Point

The chasing of perfection not only disrupts the dynamics of teamwork but can also lead to leadership burnout. As expectations escalate unchecked, leaders often find themselves stretched to their limits. Striving for an ideal that is inherently unattainable can leave them emotionally exhausted, leading to burnout.

Mark Thompson, a well-respected leader in the finance sector, also fell victim to the perilous pursuit of perfection. "I would work long hours and pour over reports, convinced that if I could eliminate every error, I would be regarded as the best leader there was," he reflects. However, what ensued was a damaging cycle of stress and relentless dedication. Mark's identity became intertwined with his role—a toxic amalgamation of work and self-worth.

Eventually, after an intense project fueled by weeks of sleepless nights, he hit a wall. "I collapsed one evening after a meeting—I couldn't focus on basic tasks; my mind felt like it was on fire," he admits. It was only after his health was jeopardized that he began to realize the toll of his perfectionism and the necessity for a healthier relationship with his work and leadership.

Discontent Within Teams

When leaders obsessively chase perfection, the resulting discontent can significantly affect team dynamics. Employees may feel pressured to conform to unrealistic standards, leading to disengagement, frustration, and decreased productivity. The high cost of perfectionism manifests in employee turnover, as talented individuals flee environments where their creativity and autonomy are stifled by an overly critical atmosphere.

Jane Whitaker, a project manager in the tech industry, experienced first-hand the effects of her perfection-oriented leader. "We had a supervisor who was brilliant in many aspects, but she had an unhealthy obsession with details. Every little thing had to be perfect, which made us all afraid to act—for fear our actions would not meet her standards." Jane describes the team's struggle to maintain motivation under such circumstances.

"I remember a situation where I received a positive review for a project, yet she zeroed in on a minor detail I had overlooked," she continues. This tendency fostered a toxic culture where employees avoided taking initiatives. "We were just going through the motions rather than innovating. It became a cycle of mediocrity under the guise of perfection."

The Shift Towards Embracing Imperfection

Gradually, leaders like Melissa and Mark began to understand the liberating power of embracing imperfections. They recognized that fostering a culture of psychological safety, where team members could express themselves without fear of criticism, was essential to true leadership growth. Acceptance of mistakes served as a catalyst for feedback, learning, and ultimately, personal growth.

Melissa reflects on the turning point in her leadership journey. "After realizing the impact of my perfectionism, I set out to create a safe space for my team. I began sharing my own mistakes and lessons learned openly, inviting others to do the same." This change did not come easily. Many team members were initially hesitant to break free from the grip of perfectionism ingrained in their culture.

"We had to actively practice embracing imperfections together," she explains. Gradually, team members began to share setbacks in meetings. This culture shift not only invigorated creativity but also fostered deeper relationships rooted in mutual support. "It was refreshing to see how quickly trust rebuilt when we showed our human sides," adds Melissa.

Mark's journey echoed similar sentiments. Once he stepped back from the obsession with perfection, he realized that vulnerability was a powerful connector. "I started involving my team in decision-making, encouraging them to take risks. Instead of just aiming for flawless execution, I wanted our projects to reflect authenticity," he shares. Through this new approach, the creativity in their strategies flourished, leading to innovative solutions for complex problems.

Lessons Learned

1. **Acknowledge Imperfection**: Embracing imperfections doesn't equate to lowering standards; rather, it fosters an environment conducive to learning. Melissa notes, "When you accept that mistakes happen, you create a culture that learns from them instead of fearing them." Leaders must recognize the benefits of allowing both themselves and their teams to be imperfect in order to innovate.

2. **Foster Open Communication**: Mark highlights that establishing a culture of psychological safety is paramount. "We need to promote open dialogue about challenges and setbacks, allowing everyone to contribute without fear of retribution." Creating space for constructive feedback nurtures creativity and provides avenues for continuous improvement.

3. **Reframe Success**: Redefining what success looks like can profoundly alter team dynamics. Moving from a narrow definition based on flawless execution toward measuring growth and learning from experiences allows leaders and their teams to celebrate progress.

4. **Practice Self-Compassion**: For many perfectionists, self-criticism is the norm; however, a shift towards self-compassion is essential for long-term growth. Melissa emphasizes, "It's vital to treat ourselves with kindness and acceptance in our moments of imperfections to model this behavior for our teams." Allowing space for vulnerability cultivates a more authentic leadership style.

5. **Embrace Continuous Learning**: Perfectionists often regard themselves as the final authority, stifling their growth. Mark encourages leaders to engage regularly in educational opportunities to expand their understanding and develop their skillsets, asserting, "When we make learning a priority, we focus on improvement rather than the unattainable goal of perfection."

A Path Forward

Leaders who commit to rejecting the shackles of perfectionism are empowered to nurture a healthier work environment. With gratitude, Melissa states, "Reassessing my approach to leadership has transformed my life, my teams' dynamic, and ultimately, our success." Reflexive practices surrounding imperfections can breed resilience and resourcefulness in teams, creating an atmosphere where creativity thrives and innovation becomes commonplace.

Through shared narratives, the path of embracing imperfection may unfold as leaders navigate through their own challenges. As we move forward, it's vital to honor the stories of those who dared to acknowledge their fallibility. In doing so, we redefine the essence of leadership, prioritizing authenticity and connection over an elusive ideal of perfection.

In closing, the shadow of perfectionism looms over many leaders, threatening to stifle their true potential. However, by recognizing its limitations and embracing imperfections as integral to the human experience, leaders can foster environments rich with learning, growth, and innovation. Through authenticity, vulnerability, and shared experiences, a new era of leadership can emerge—one grounded in strength, flexibility, and above all, humanity.

The Fallibility of Leaders

In the world of leadership, the prevailing narrative often glorifies those who exhibit strength, decisiveness, and an unwavering commitment to excellence. We are quick to praise leaders who seem to have the answers, who navigate challenges with the skill of a seasoned captain steering a ship through stormy seas. However, beneath this polished exterior lurks a profound truth: leaders are, at their core, human. They are fallible, imperfect beings who grapple with uncertainties, make mistakes, and face the trials and errors that come with the territory. This subchapter delves into the complex reality of leadership fallibility, encouraging reflection and cultivating a culture where vulnerability is embraced rather than shunned.

The reality is that even the most revered leaders have stumbled. Their journeys are marked not only by triumphs but also by failures that often provide the most valuable lessons. One notable example is former General Electric CEO Jack Welch, who was celebrated for transforming GE into a powerhouse of profitability and efficiency. Welch was known for his "rank and yank" performance evaluation system, where the bottom 10% of employees were let go annually. While this approach initially earned him respect for his ruthless pursuit of excellence, it ultimately led to a toxic workplace culture characterized by fear and mistrust. Employees began to see each other not as collaborators but as competitors, which stifled innovation and hindered communication. This example illustrates how a strong desire to achieve can, when taken to extremes, result in devastating consequences for team morale and engagement.

Another powerful case study is that of Elizabeth Holmes, the founder of Theranos, whose vision of revolutionizing healthcare through innovative blood-testing technology captured the world's imagination. Initially, Holmes was lauded as a visionary leader, admired for her ambition and charisma. However, the company's dream quickly unraveled when it was revealed that their technology was flawed and that the results were often inaccurate. The cult-like atmosphere surrounding Theranos was cultivated by Holmes, who discouraged dissent and stifled critical feedback from employees who had concerns about the technology's reliability. The fallout was catastrophic, resulting in criminal charges against Holmes and the eventual disintegration of Theranos. This story serves as a cautionary tale, reminding leaders of the importance of humility and the necessity of welcoming dissenting voices in pursuit of a shared vision.

Perhaps one of the most relatable aspects of leadership fallibility is the concept of hubris. Overconfidence can lead even the most capable leaders to make critical errors in judgment. Take the case of former Nokia CEO Stephen Elop, who infamously declared the company would no longer rely on its dominance in the mobile phone market, opting instead for Microsoft's Windows Phone platform. The decision, made amid rising competition from Apple and Android devices, proved disastrous. Nokia lost its market share and struggled to regain a foothold in the smartphone space, ultimately leading to its acquisition by Microsoft. Elop's overconfidence in a strategy that disregarded consumer preferences serves as a stark reminder of the dangers of ignoring feedback and failing to adapt to evolving landscapes.

Reflecting on the stories of leaders like Welch, Holmes, and Elop highlights the crucial need for self-awareness and the acknowledgment of vulnerabilities in leadership. The irony is that genuine strength does not stem from pretending to be infallible; instead, it arises from recognizing one's limitations and embracing the very human experience of making mistakes. Such acknowledgment can inspire a culture of openness within organizations, enabling teams to learn from failures and ultimately drive innovation.

This culture of openness starts with leaders modeling vulnerability. When leaders share their own experiences of failure, they signal to employees that it's acceptable to be imperfect and to seek help when needed. Consider the story of Howard Schultz, the former CEO of Starbucks, who openly spoke about his struggles with leadership during the company's early years. Schultz recounted how he faced numerous challenges, including losing the company's focus on its core values as it expanded rapidly. Rather than hiding these setbacks, he used them as opportunities to reassess and refocus Starbucks' mission. This honest reflection not only strengthened his leadership but also reinforced the company's commitment to its ideals. As a result, Starbucks re-established its connection with customers and employees alike, showcasing the power of vulnerability in fostering resilience and unity.

Welcoming mistakes does not equate to tolerating mediocrity; instead, it reflects a commitment to learning and growth. Adopting a growth mindset, as championed by psychologist Carol Dweck, can be transformative. Leaders who embrace a growth mindset view challenges as opportunities for development. They understand that learning often comes from setbacks, and they cultivate environments where employees can experiment, innovate, and reflect on their experiences without fear of repercussions. The organization becomes a living entity, thriving on collaboration and mutual respect.

One leader who embodies this philosophy is Satya Nadella of Microsoft, who took the helm during a challenging period for the tech giant. Nadella recognized the need to change the company culture from one focused on competition to one centered on collaboration and learning. By fostering a growth mindset, he encouraged employees to embrace experimentation and accept that failure is part of the journey toward success. Under Nadella's leadership, Microsoft saw a remarkable resurgence, with renewed innovation, higher employee morale, and ultimately, significant financial growth. His approach serves as a testament to the idea that acknowledging fallibility can lead to remarkable transformations.

Of course, cultivating a culture of openness is not without its challenges. Leaders may struggle with the fear of how vulnerability will be perceived. The pressures of maintaining an image, especially in competitive environments, can create tensions between authenticity and perception. It's essential for leaders to confront this fear head-on, understanding that their authenticity can strengthen rather than weaken their leadership standing.

As leaders embark on this journey toward vulnerability, practical actions can help facilitate a culture of learning from failure. First, they must encourage transparent communication within teams. Establishing regular check-ins and debrief sessions after projects can create safe spaces for employees to voice concerns and share lessons learned. These conversations nurture an environment that values feedback and collective growth.

Additionally, celebrating failures as opportunities for learning is a critical aspect of breaking down the stigma associated with mistakes. Organizations can establish a "failure wall," where teams can share their missteps and the lessons learned from them. By reframing failure as an integral part of the innovation process, leaders reinforce the value of experimentation and discourage the fear associated with taking risks.

Another important facet of fostering a culture of openness is providing access to professional development resources. Leaders should prioritize training that equips employees with the skills they need to cope with challenges effectively. Workshops on resilience, emotional intelligence, and feedback can empower employees to take ownership of their growth. When team members feel invested in their personal and professional development, they become more likely to embrace vulnerability and acknowledge their own limitations.

It's also essential to model vulnerability at all levels of leadership. Senior leaders must be willing to share their own experiences, including mistakes, with their teams. This transparency fosters trust and encourages others within the organization to do the same. When junior employees see executives acknowledge their flaws and the lessons they derive from them, they feel empowered to step forward as well.

As we explore the fallibility of leaders, it becomes clear that the journey is not merely about identifying missteps but also about actively transforming a culture rooted in growth and learning. Leaders should encourage their teams to embrace challenges, view tensions as fertile ground for growth, and celebrate the resilience that emerges from hardships.

Ultimately, the fallibility of leaders connects to their humanity. By acknowledging their vulnerabilities, successful leaders cultivate an environment where openness is cherished, and innovation thrives. The narratives of those who have navigated their shortcomings with grace provide a roadmap for aspiring leaders, reminding us that growth and learning are continuous processes. As organizations embrace this understanding, they empower their teams to acknowledge their fallibility, driving a culture of openness, learning, and collective achievement.

In conclusion, it becomes evident that the myth of ideal leadership is not in creating flawless leaders but in embracing the imperfections that make us human. By exploring the stories of those who have faced failure, reflecting on our own vulnerabilities, and fostering a culture where mistakes are viewed as opportunities for growth, we create environments that not only nurture innovation but also inspire resilience. Therefore, as leaders, let us unite in the understanding that the path to sustainable growth lies not in the avoidance of mistakes but in our willingness to learn from them and support one another in the journey ahead.

CHAPTER TWO

TOLERANCE: THE DOUBLE-EDGED SWORD

The Silent Boardroom

In the heart of many organizations lies the corporate boardroom—a space often revered as the epicenter of decision-making and strategic vision. Yet, for all its prestige, this room can also be a place where silence reigns supreme, a vast expanse of unspoken words and unresolved issues. Here, the notion of tolerance can morph into a double-edged sword, where the pursuit of harmony inadvertently stifles essential dialogues that could promote growth, innovation, and a stronger team dynamic.

Imagine a boardroom filled with senior executives, each member seated around a polished mahogany table, the air thick with unexpressed thoughts and concerns. The tension is palpable; the agenda is set to discuss declining sales figures. As the Chief Executive Officer presents the data, eyes dart around the room, avoiding direct contact, unable—or perhaps unwilling—to speak their minds. Ideas that could breathe life into stagnation remain unvoiced, and what could have been an opportunity for improvement turns into a missed chance to address underlying problems.

The outdated adage, "if you can't say something nice, don't say anything at all," may echo within the walls of this corporate haven. However, stifling dissenting voices or avoiding difficult conversations often leads to greater harm. It builds a culture of complacency, where unresolved issues fester under the surface, creating an insidious environment that discourages innovation and critical thinking. This scenario serves as a cautionary tale, a reminder of the thin line between fostering a congenial atmosphere and encouraging necessary discussions.

To illustrate how tolerance can eclipse dialogue, consider the case of a manufacturing company grappling with quality control issues. The boardroom is filled with representatives from various departments: production, quality assurance, sales, and marketing. The floor is open for discussion, yet an invisible barrier prevents frank conversations. While the manufacturing director has pressing concerns over production defects that could tarnish the company's reputation, the sales team is anxious about facing clients with negative news. To maintain harmony, both sides sidestep the issue, leading to a collective avoidance that ultimately impacts the organization.

In this scenario, the manufacturing director might have felt that bringing up the quality control problems could be viewed as antagonistic, risking a confrontation that could disrupt the perceived tranquility among his peers. The sales team, too, may have been reluctant to highlight the defects for fear of damaging relationships with the board members entrenched in maintaining a positive organizational image. As a result, a critical conversation concerning quality standards, accountability, and the ramifications of unresolved issues never surfaces.

That boardroom, which could have been a crucible for constructive dialogue, has thus transformed into a silent arena where the danger of complacency hides in plain sight. Leaders often assume that silence is synonymous with agreement, neglecting the reality that unspoken dissent breeds resentment and confusion. Silence is not silence; it is a decision, and in many cases, a detrimental one.

Delving deeper into the ramifications of a silent boardroom, we can explore how the fear of conflict affects leaders' capacity to facilitate open dialogue. The prevailing ethos of tolerance for divergent views can morph into a reluctance to confront issues that could create tension. Leaders may believe that by avoiding uncomfortable discussions, they are preserving camaraderie—the illusion of unity—that fills the air with a false sense of security. This desire for harmony often overlooks the critical role conflict plays in driving innovation and healthy competition among teams.

Take, for example, a tech startup experiencing rapid growth in its early stages. The founders and the leadership team, buoyed by their initial successes, embrace a culture of tolerance. Decisions are made rapidly, with little room for dissent. As the company scales, however, the demands and challenges become more complex, and the lack of constructive conflict leads to a stagnation of ideas. Team members hesitantly voice concerns, fearing that their input might shatter the camaraderie established from the start. Consequently, what could have been strategic discussions about refining the product become muted as everyone nods in silent agreement, hoping to avoid rocking the boat.

Without allowing for critical voices to emerge, this startup risks not only its innovative edge but also its ability to adapt to evolving market needs. Tolerance in this context suppresses creative solutions, stifles dialogue, and culminates in a culture resistant to change. Conflict, when addressed constructively, often brings out essential insights that lead to evolution and improvement. Therefore, a boardroom where silence prevails ultimately does a disservice to all involved.

Furthermore, as boardrooms drift into silence, the consequences extend beyond the immediate discussions. Employees may witness the avoidance of critical topics and become discouraged from pursuing open conversations, perpetuating a cycle of silence. A lingering issue that remains unaddressed may morph into a larger organizational crisis, leading to reputational damage and disengaged teams. Employees who believe their voices have no value may disengage. Their once-enthusiastic contributions become muted, resulting in a loss of valuable perspectives and potential solutions that could benefit the organization.

We also have to recognize that silence in the boardroom can be more than just a cultural impediment; it can manifest as a tangible risk to the organization's bottom line. Consider a company facing significant competition in its market sector. Decisions about product development, pricing strategies, and market positioning become increasingly critical. At that moment, open dialogue and the willingness to challenge the status quo are paramount.

However, when tolerance becomes the prevailing ideal, boards may limit the opportunities for challenging conversations due to fear of divisiveness. The harsh reality sets in: while the leadership may succeed in creating a congenial environment, they risk becoming an echo chamber, where all present agree for the sake of civility, leading to stagnation and failure to anticipate market shifts.

This box of complacency can be illustrated through the experience of a veteran board member who understood the importance of dialogue. Despite the prevailing culture, he continually sought to elicit honest feedback from his peers. Each time he brought up a difficult topic, he noticed the tension in the room transform into cautious engagement. By giving others space to voice their concerns without judgment, he demonstrated how effective facilitation could transform a silent room into a space for dynamic conversation.

Implicitly, he cultivated a sense of accountability, encouraging others to relinquish their fear of reprisal. This shift underscored an essential paradox: while an organization may strive for harmony through tolerance, the silence that ensues can be more damaging than any discord that may arise from honest discussions.

The scenarios presented so far highlight the importance of leadership in creating an environment where dialogue thrives, yet fostering open conversations demands conscious efforts. Leaders must actively model the behaviors they wish to see within their teams. Transparency, accountability, and vulnerability are crucial traits that will help dismantle the hesitance that often silences individuals in the boardroom. This requires recognizing that tolerance does not mean avoidance—rather, it must be the foundation for respectful discourse.

To break the cycle of silence, leaders could consider implementing frameworks that prioritize constructive conflict. For example, establishing guidelines for engaging in difficult conversations can provide a safety net for team members who fear objection or refutation. When a structure is in place to address discrepancies, discrepancies no longer become threats but opportunities for dialogue and collaboration.

Organizations may also benefit from naming and normalizing conflict as a part of their strategic discussions. Through facilitated workshops or strategic retreats, leaders can practice having uncomfortable conversations in a supportive atmosphere, developing the skills necessary to engage in tough dialogues with confidence. Instead of letting issues fester beneath the surface, improving conflict management becomes crucial to unlocking potential and fostering a healthier organizational culture.

Ultimately, the path to a thriving boardroom lies in acknowledging that discomfort is a natural part of collaboration, and silence does not equal agreement. Leaders are called to create forums where thoughts and opinions flow freely, establishing transparency as the hallmark of their leadership philosophy. It also means being willing to challenge their tolerance threshold, tempering it with a commitment to fostering feedback. Acknowledging that clashing perspectives can yield transformative insights is paramount.

As corporate leaders reflect on their practice within the boardroom, they must ask themselves: How can I challenge silence? How can I promote a culture that thrives on dialogue instead of harmony? These questions mark the beginning of a journey toward a more engaged and dynamic organization—a boardroom where tolerance serves as the foundation for candid conversations.

In closing, the image of the silent boardroom starkly contrasts with the vibrant discourse required for powerful leadership and effective teamwork. While tolerance undoubtedly plays a role in guiding organizational dynamics, it is crucial for leaders to navigate the balance between maintaining collegiality and fostering the dialogue necessary for growth. By embracing confrontational discussions, leaders can propel their organizations forward, avoiding the pitfalls of complacency and nurturing a culture where innovation flourishes above all else.

Examples of Courageous Conflict

In an era defined by rapid change and constant competition, the importance of fostering a culture that encourages courageous conflict cannot be overstated. While conventional wisdom often promotes the idea that harmony within teams is the ultimate goal, the most innovative and effective organizations understand that constructive conflict can serve as a catalyst for growth and improvement. This subchapter explores a tapestry of stories featuring leaders who dared to engage in challenging dialogues, challenging the status quo and driving their organizations toward profound progress.

One notable example is the case of a global technology firm, **InnoTech**, where a fundamental shift in leadership approach created waves of positive change. The company had long been known for its innovative products but was experiencing a decline in market share due to an increasing number of competitors. After witnessing the decline, the new CEO, **Rebecca Lane**, recognized that the lack of open dialogue among the leadership team was stifling innovation. She initiated "innovation sessions," structured meetings designated for the sole purpose of addressing dissenting opinions.

During one notable session, a junior product manager named **Chris** raised concerns about a new product line that everyone else had largely endorsed. **Chris's** perspective was born from his direct interactions with customers, who expressed dissatisfaction with certain features. Instead of dismissing the concerns, Rebecca encouraged an open debate, asking everyone to share their viewpoints, regardless of rank. As the conversation evolved, it became clear that the issue was systemic; several others felt similarly but had been hesitant to speak up.

Through this courageous act of instigating conflict, Rebecca not only validated **Chris's** concerns but also elicited a range of opinions that challenged the initial product strategy. By creating a safe environment for dialogue, Rebecca's leadership fostered a culture of innovation that ultimately led to a revamped version of the product line, which became the company's top seller within months. This example highlights how embracing courageous conflict can salvage a struggling organization, turning dissent into a decisive advantage.

Another compelling narrative comes from **Tread Lightly**, an environmentally-conscious footwear company that was on the verge of losing its mission-driven values as it scaled. **Thomas**, the CTO, overheard conversations in the hallways expressing frustration over the lack of ethics in manufacturing choices, particularly around sourcing materials. **Thomas**, a firm believer in transparency, recognized the need for a dedicated forum to discuss such critical issues openly.

He organized a series of **"Values Workshops,"** where employees could discuss ethical dilemmas in a focused manner. At one particularly heated workshop, two groups emerged: one group advocated for cheaper materials to maximize profits while the other insisted on sticking to the environmentally friendly options that had defined the brand. Instead of insisting on consensus, Thomas encouraged passionate debate, allowing employees to express their fears, hopes, and motivations behind their positions.

The result was a powerful resolution that integrated ideas from both sides. By addressing the conflict directly, the company redefined its supply chain strategy—not only maintaining its ethical standards but also discovering more innovative and cost-effective sourcing solutions. Employees left the workshop feeling heard and valued, and morale soared.

Stories of courageous conflict are not confined to private enterprises or new startups; they are equally relevant in public sectors and non-profits. Take the case of a large urban school district where the superintendent, **Dr. Maria Lopez**, faced increasing pressure over declining student performance metrics. It was clear that issues ran deeper than mere funding. Teachers felt unheard and frustrated by administrative decisions that seemed disconnected from their realities in the classroom.

Recognizing the growing discord, Dr. Lopez held a series of open forums throughout the community, inviting teachers, parents, and even students to voice their concerns openly. The discussions were often contentious, with varying opinions and experiences laid bare. However, the conflicts that arose from these dialogues ultimately painted a more comprehensive picture of the root causes behind the performance issues.

One particular instance saw a high school history teacher, **James**, passionately argue against district protocols that he believed stifled creativity in lesson planning. Instead of minimizing the criticisms, Dr. Lopez reframed the conversation by acknowledging the challenges while facilitating further dialogue on potential solutions. This not only empowered **James** but also encouraged other educators to share their experiences, enriching the collective understanding of the systemic barriers that limited effective teaching.

Dr. Lopez utilized this moment of courageous conflict to develop targeted initiatives that bore direct relevance to educators' realities, ultimately leading the district to revamp curriculum standards and professional development. The district began to see improved student outcomes, and more importantly, teachers felt rejuvenated and engaged as active participants in the decision-making process.

Courageous conflict can also find meaningful representation in collaborative teams within large corporations. Consider the case study of **Unity Corp**, a multinational corporation specializing in software development. The company had cultivated a reputation for its vibrant team culture, yet a noticeable stagnation had swept through its innovation teams. Internal surveys revealed a widespread sense of complacency that leadership struggled to identify and address.

In response, the Chief Innovation Officer, **Elena Wang**, took an unconventional approach by instituting **"Disruption Days,"** where employees were encouraged to challenge existing projects and voice their concerns without fear of retribution. During the first Disruption Day, a developer named **Martin** boldly critiqued the focus on an underperforming app that the company had invested heavily in.

While this revelation sparked initial defensiveness among project leaders, **Elena** expertly redirected the energy toward problem-solving. She facilitated breakout sessions, which allowed employees from various departments to think creatively about solutions. The results were astounding. Employees developed a comprehensive plan to either pivot from the project or fully revamp its direction. Not only did this engagement result in renewed energy around the software's development, but it also ignited a cultural shift where employees felt empowered to openly discuss and challenge existing projects. This cultivation of open conflict not only salvaged key product lines but also enhanced the company's innovative practices moving forward.

It's essential to emphasize that these examples are not anomalies; they represent the power of courageous conflict when effectively harnessed.

However, creating an environment where constructive criticism flourishes requires more than just willingness from leaders. It necessitates an intentional strategy that prioritizes communication, vulnerability, and trust.

To cultivate such an environment, leaders should:

1. **Model Vulnerability:** Leaders should openly acknowledge their own mistakes and uncertainties. By doing so, they pave the way for others to feel safe in voicing their opinions and concerns.

2. **Encourage Diverse Perspectives:** Leaders must actively seek out differing viewpoints, especially from those who may be marginalized or hesitant to speak. This ensures a rich discourse and fosters innovation through varied ideas.

3. **Choose the Right Setting:** Designating safe spaces for dialogue—such as team retreats, workshops, or dedicated meetings—can help frame discussions around conflict in productive ways.

4. **Frame Conflict as an Opportunity:** Educating teams to perceive conflict as a vehicle for progress rather than a threat can shift their mindset. Leaders should regularly discuss the benefits of open dialogue.

5. **Follow Through:** Lastly, leaders must demonstrate that embarked conflicts yield tangible outcomes. By implementing suggestions made during courageous conversations, leaders reinforce the value of dialogue.

The stories shared throughout this subchapter underscore the theme that tolerance should never supersede the necessity for honesty and open dialogue. Embracing challenging conversations does pose a risk—conflict can be uncomfortable, and dissent may lead to tensions. Yet, failing to engage in these discussions can produce far greater risks, as witnessed in organizations that opt for silence over speaking out. Courageous conflict offers a pathway to innovation, promoting collective decision-making and empowering teams to thrive.

As leaders reflect upon their journeys, they must recognize the significance of creating a culture that champions not only tolerance but the courage to engage in difficult discussions. For therein lies the heart of true progress, where innovation flourishes, and boundless possibilities emerge.

The Fog of Tolerance

In the world of leadership, tolerance is often held up as a virtue. Leaders are instructed to foster inclusive environments where everyone can contribute without fear of judgment or reprisal. Yet, as the notion of tolerance evolves into something akin to unchecked acceptance, organizations can find themselves enveloped in a dense fog. This fog obscures critical issues, leaving teams adrift without direction, purpose, or clarity.

Picture this: a corporate team, once vibrant with ideas and collaborative spirit, becomes a subdued assembly of heads bowed low under the weight of invisible pressures. Meetings that once sparkled with creativity devolve into monotonous recitations of the status quo. Staff members tread cautiously, careful not to disturb the fragile balance that excessive tolerance has wrought. Here, silence reigns supreme, and the vibrant exchange of ideas has suffocated under an oppressive blanket of complacency.

As we delve deeper into the effects of this fog, we explore various case studies that exemplify how tolerance, when amplified past a healthy limit, mutates into its own oppressive entity. One notable example is a prominent tech organization, lauded for its progressive culture and inclusive policy initiatives. At first glance, the company's leadership team appeared to embody the quintessential progressive mindset — diversity of thought was cherished, and dissent, celebrated. However, as time marched on, an unsettling trend began to surface.

Dissenters found their voices muted, unseen forces pressuring them to conform to the majority view. Efforts to promote tolerance inadvertently fostered an environment ripe for mediocrity, where critical feedback was sacrificed on the altar of harmony. Leadership refrained from addressing concerns, fearing that confrontation would disrupt the carefully curated facade of unity. Decisions made in the boardroom became devoid of scrutiny, and the company began to experience significant setbacks — diminished innovation, a sharp decline in team morale, and increasing turnover rates. Managers were hesitant to voice their opinions, and as a result, teams were left stagnating.

When leaders indulge this fog of tolerance, they risk blinding themselves to the very problems that could derail their organizations. The lack of feedback loops, which are essential for growth and development, creates a breeding ground for discontent to simmer beneath the surface. Without mechanisms for constructive criticism, employees have no outlets for their frustrations, and disillusionment festers. The most troubling aspect of this scenario is that everyone involved — from the highest-ranking executives to entry-level employees — may not even realize this environment is taking shape. The insidious nature of excessive tolerance leaves many unwitting participants trapped within its confines, unaware that they have lost sight of their organizational vision.

The consequences of this unchecked tolerance extend beyond mere dissatisfaction. The lack of engagement within teams can lead to an erosion of trust, which is fundamental to any organization's success. Trust formed through open dialogue, constructive conflict, and mutual respect can evaporate when the pressure not to disagree becomes an unspoken rule. Employees start to withdraw and disengage, believing their voices no longer matter. Innovation stagnates, and eventually, organizations find themselves floundering amid changing market conditions, unable to pivot, evolve, or compete in a landscape that grows more competitive by the day.

Consider, for instance, the narrative of a mid-sized manufacturing company that once excelled in producing high-quality products. Upon initiation of a progressive 'tolerance-first' policy, the leadership team celebrated its intention to invite more diverse thoughts into decision-making processes. Yet, as tolerance tightened its grip, dissent ceased to exist. Employees avoided raising concerns about production inefficiencies, fearing punishment or being ostracized for challenging authority. As operational issues grew, the company's output dwindled, and the once well-respected brand unraveled. In its quest for harmony, the leadership failed to hold itself accountable — choosing to ignore the warning signs that would have prompted necessary change. The fog of tolerance led to blind spots that no amount of optimism could rectify.

Over time, tales of lost liberties within the workplace became commonplace; teams were captivated in this fog, experiencing morale depletion that slowly dripped into exodus. This drop-off resulted in a loss of valuable insights and experiences that would have otherwise contributed to innovation and agility. An organization is only as strong as its people, and when voices are silenced, the ability to harness collective insights diminishes.

In understanding how to combat this challenge, we must grapple with the importance of awareness and accountability in leadership. A crucial first step is fostering an environment that encourages open dialogues even, and especially, when the conversations are uncomfortable. Leaders must embrace a concept often labeled as 'radical candor,' fostering dialogues where individuals can thrive despite divergent opinions. This transformation does not occur overnight and requires unwavering commitment to the process.

The leadership of organizations ensnared in the fog of tolerance may ask themselves: "How can we cultivate a culture that values open feedback rather than one that inadvertently silences it?" One compelling answer lies in establishing clear protocols for communication and accountability. Regularly scheduled check-ins between teams, management, and leaders help create opportunities for evaluation of team dynamics and performance. This practice can help illuminate potential issues that would otherwise remain in the fog.

Moreover, conducting anonymous feedback surveys can serve as valuable instruments. They offer employees a safe channel to express concerns that may be too daunting to bring up in person. This, however, must be paired with a commitment to act on the feedback received, with transparent communication throughout the process regarding how the organization plans to address the concerns. Teams must witness the tangible outcomes of their voices carrying weight, or they risk becoming disillusioned and retreating further into the fog.

Frequent opportunities for reflection can also catalyze growth. Leaders should encourage team members to examine their interactions critically. Workshops focused on conflict resolution, effective communication, and team-building exercises can dismantle existing barriers and facilitate trust. When employees observe their leaders demonstrating vulnerability and a commitment to growth — admitting when they err and pivoting from their mistakes — they receive an unobstructed view of what open dialogue looks like. Beyond merely observing these practices, leaders must actively promote a culture of accountability for themselves and their teams, demonstrating that no one is above the collective responsibility of the organization.

Further, leaders must recognize the role they play in perpetuating the fog, understanding that they set the tone for the organizational culture. Displaying traits of humility and self-awareness empowers team members to offer their candid perspectives without fearing retribution. When leaders showcase how to embrace constructive criticism, they lay the groundwork for an environment that celebrates diverse inputs and makes individuals feel valued.

Providing mentorship opportunities can also serve as a buffer against the toxic fog. Establishing mentorship programs enables junior employees to connect with seasoned leaders, fostering relationships where individuals can seek guidance and share personal experiences. Moreover, they can create platforms for those less experienced to feel empowered in raising concerns and sharing ideas, ultimately breaking the cycle of silence.

As the fog of tolerance thickens, the threat of discontent grows, and the consequences become more dire. It complicates the already intricate web of workplace dynamics, blinding leaders to the very fissures in their organizational structure. The solution rests in shifting cultural norms within organizations—creating a framework that honors open discussions while upholding accountability, thereby ejecting the fog that obscures clarity.

While many leaders would like to believe they have fostered a culture of tolerance without incident, the true test lies in moments of conflict. An organization that confronts challenges directly is one that possesses the potential for long-lasting growth. It is through grappling with discord that teams learn to innovate and create solutions. These moments, often uncomfortable, become opportunities for deeper connection and collaboration. Through shared struggle, teams solidify their foundational bonds — an invaluable element within an effective organizational ecosystem.

One successful approach to combat the fog of tolerance can be found in organizations that prioritarily structure accountability into their developmental frameworks. For example, a prominent consulting firm embarked on transforming its traditionally hierarchical environment into one characterized by egalitarian feedback cycles. This involved training teams to provide constructive criticism in a manner that was both respectful and empowering. The result was a cultural metamorphosis with a noticeable decline in frustration and an unexpected surge in innovative projects. Staff worked collaboratively, producing work that exceeded previous standards as the fog cleared.

The ultimate aim should be to progress from mere tolerance to genuine acceptance, where differences are not only recognized but celebrated. By creating robust communication channels and establishing trust, leaders can lay the groundwork for more productive conflict engagement. Diffusing the fog removes barriers to visibility within teams, creating much-needed transparency that enhances accountability and empowers individuals. Organizations thrive when they engage in dialogue, creativity, and innovation — using feedback as a catalyst for positive growth rather than a hindrance to unity.

Ultimately, as we reconsider what tolerance means in the context of leadership, we must acknowledge the thin line between mindless acceptance and the cultivation of a dialogue-rich culture. Tolerance without scrutiny transforms into its own threat, clouding vision and weakening structure. It is the role of effective leaders to illuminate this path, teaching their teams to navigate through the fog toward clarity, trust, and a shared vision. In recognizing the role of active awareness and accountability, leaders must advocate for a departure from the passive acceptance of the status quo and a movement toward dynamic engagement where every voice is not only heard but valued.

As we conclude this exploration of the fog of tolerance, leaders are reminded that embracing constructive conflict invigorates organizations with potential. Those willing to uplift voices amid the mists are the transformational leaders fostering resilient teams eager to innovate and collaborate. In the end, it is those dynamic dialogues that can light the way out of the fog and onto the path of progress.

CHAPTER THREE

WHEN PRIDE PLUNGES INTO ARROGANCE

The Rise of Arrogance

In the landscape of leadership, pride often emerges as a double-edged sword. For many leaders, pride serves as the fuel that drives them toward remarkable achievements, propelling them to take bold risks and envision lofty goals. It can instill confidence, inspiring those around them to rally behind a shared vision. However, when pride spirals into arrogance, it manifests as a dangerous distortion, undermining the very foundations of leadership itself. This transformation can diminish trust, stifle innovation, and ultimately lead to organizational failure.

To understand how pride can morph into arrogance, we first need to explore the nuances of pride in leadership. Consider the story of Sarah, an accomplished CEO of a rapidly growing tech startup. When Sarah first launched her company, her pride stemmed from her unwavering belief in her innovative product. Fueled by her confidence, she led her team to achieve early successes, garnering significant investments and attracting top talent. Her determinative nature forged a clear path forward, instilling a sense of purpose in her employees.

Yet, as the company grew, so did Sarah's ego. With every milestone reached, the admiration from peers and stakeholders fueled her sense of superiority. Gradually, she began to dismiss critical feedback, as she perceived challenges not as opportunities for learning but as personal attacks on her vision. Her once-collaborative leadership style shifted; team members felt increasingly marginalized if their perspectives conflicted with her opinions. As she actively curated a culture that worshipped her ideation, creativity dwindled among her team.

The result was a stagnation within the company. Brilliant minds that had once contributed dynamic ideas now hesitated to speak up. They worried that presenting alternative viewpoints could trigger Sarah's ire, driving them further from her inner circle. What had begun as a company marked by aspiration morphed into a toxic echo chamber, where dissent was stifled, and the illusion of overarching stability reigned.

Sarah's story is not an anomaly but a template that recounts the trajectory of many leaders who allow pride to cloud their judgment. When confidence crosses into entitlement, it breeds myopia—the inability to see one's flaws because they are enshrouded in a veil of self-importance. Furthermore, leaders who cultivate an arrogance-fueled culture often find themselves facing unexpected consequences, as the very talent that propelled their success quietly disengages, leaving a vacuum of innovation in its wake.

Another illustrative case is that of Martin, a former head of sales at a major corporation. He was known for his strategic acumen and had a history of surpassing quarterly targets. Initially, his proud demeanor inspired his team, who viewed him as a visionary. However, as Martin continued to outperform his peers, his humility eroded. He began to isolate himself, cutting off feedback channels and relying only on the advice of a select few whom he deemed aligned with his vision.

One pivotal moment came during a crucial client presentation. Martin's reliance on a narrow feedback loop meant he had not considered the client's evolving needs. When the presentation flopped, it not only cost the company the account but also damaged relationships with several other clients who saw the presentation as a reflection of the company's quality.

In both Sarah and Martin's narratives, we witness how success can lead to a dangerous misconception: that pride alone will sustain future victories. The rise of arrogance is often gradual, masquerading as self-confidence. Yet, the moment leaders treat feedback as noise rather than a vital instrument for growth, they pave the way for their downfall.

Ignorance of dissent breeds a culture devoid of accountability. This lack of scrutiny can manifest in disastrous decision-making. For instance, let's examine Jerry, the CEO of a prominent automotive firm. Jerry had a track record of revolutionizing the industry with sustainable vehicle technology, making him a celebrated figure within the industry. His ego, however, demanded constant validation. Over time, it led to a culture where only those who echoed Jerry's grand visions received recognition.

When environmental regulations changed, his team identified the necessity for a strategic pivot to develop hybrid models. Despite numerous data reports suggesting an urgent need for adaptation, Jerry became dismissive, perceiving these insights as an affront to his prowess as an innovative leader. The ramifications were severe: competitors who embraced the change surged ahead, and Jerry's company fell significantly behind, losing both market share and the loyalty of employees who once admired him.

The turning point was a board meeting that would come to define Jerry's legacy. As the team presented information highlighting dwindling sales figures, Jerry's face flushed with indignation. He interrupted the presentation, accusing his team of defeatism while praising his past successes. The meeting ended in a tense silence, further alienating key players within the organization. They quickly lost trust in his vision and leadership, leading to a mass exodus of talent that found solace at rival companies.

Through these stories, a pattern emerges—leaders who allow pride to mutate into arrogance blind themselves to the realities their organizations face. They often surround themselves with those who affirm their beliefs while dismissing dissent. As a result, prioritizing their inflated sense of self becomes the norm, shattering the trust that is essential to teamwork and collaboration.

For leaders entrenched in prideful arrogance, the signs of decline often materialize in subtle ways initially. Project timelines slip, team morale dwindles, and innovation stalls as a culture of fear supplants one of engagement. The longer these signs are ignored, the more potent the impact becomes. Ultimately, it leads to an organizational meltdown that stems not just from poor decisions but from an inability to foster a learning environment.

This was the plight of Alex, the renowned leader of a global tech enterprise. Under his command, the company enjoyed a meteoric rise, consistently launching disruptive technologies that reshaped market landscapes. As accolades poured in, Alex's pride grew to unmanageable proportions, convincing him that his understanding of the market was unparalleled. Team members who once contributed to brainstorming sessions found their ideas silenced.

Over time, the organization became entrenched in its own echo chamber of past successes. Alex grew increasingly intolerant of differing opinions, dismissing input from anyone who dared question established norms. This arrogance was particularly evident during a product launch that failed to meet market expectations—an oversight attributed directly to the lack of diverse perspectives in the decision-making process.

In the aftermath of this failure, high-performing team members began to leave for roles at companies that encouraged creativity and open dialogue. This cascading loss of talent was a significant blow, representing not only personnel shifts but also a loss of vital knowledge and expertise. Alex's legacy became one of lost opportunity as he realized too late the cost of his pride and the arrogance it engendered.

From these examples, an undeniable truth surfaces: pride must be balanced with humility to foster resilience in leadership. When humility is overshadowed by arrogance, leaders cease to learn and grow. They become complacent, blinded by a façade of certainty, which ultimately hinders both personal and organizational progress.

Leaders need to cultivate self-awareness, allowing room for introspection and continuous growth. This practice equips them to reckon with their vulnerabilities and invites constructive feedback into their leadership approach.

Take the story of Maya, a successful CFO at a nonprofit organization. Unlike her counterparts, Maya embraced humility throughout her journey, understanding that pride in her accomplishments was only one part of the equation. She actively sought input from her team, recognizing that their diverse perspectives would yield better decision-making.

Her commitment to transparency fostered a culture where team members felt empowered to voice dissent. During critical meetings, Maya encouraged open discussions about budgetary constraints, bringing everyone into the conversation. As they navigated complex financial decisions together, the results spoke volumes: the organization flourished, and team members thrived.

The contrast between Maya's approach and those of leaders like Sarah, Martin, Jerry, and Alex is stark. While pride can serve to launch leaders forward, an absence of humility renders that momentum unsustainable. Leaders must understand that with success comes the responsibility to remain grounded in reality. Only then can they avoid the pitfalls of arrogance that lead to their undoing.

To highlight the damage that arrogance can inflict, we must also consider the ripples it sends through organizations. When arrogance dominates, accountability wanes. Employees feel less inclined to share validation and feedback, leading to a fractured workplace culture. The less people contribute, the greater the knowledge gap widens, compounding problems that could easily be mitigated through open communication.

To confront this reality head-on, leaders should actively cultivate a climate of humility. They need to lean on the collective wisdom of their teams, understanding that the strength of their organizational culture directly correlates to the extent that they can embrace a growth mindset. Leaders must recognize that they are not infallible; rather, they are part of a larger ecosystem where each member's contribution plays a role in driving success.

Ultimately, the rise of arrogance is marked by a disconnection from reality. Every leader faces a critical juncture, a point at which they must choose between reverence for their achievements or alignment with their teams. The former leads to an inflated ego that blinds leaders to emerging challenges. In contrast, the latter fosters collaboration, innovation, and resilience—the essential tenets of sustainable leadership.

As leaders reflect on their journeys, they must ask themselves some vital questions: Do I invite dissenting opinions? Am I open to feedback? Do I recognize the accomplishments of others? By embracing the vulnerability inherent in these inquiries, leaders can circumvent the perils of arrogance and cultivate enduring success through humility and shared accountability.

In closing, the trajectory of pride turning into arrogance serves as cautionary tales for present and future leaders. Through the stories of Sarah, Martin, Jerry, Alex, and the contrasting approach of Maya, we see the depths to which leadership can descend when arrogance reigns. Awareness of this paradox and the courage to embrace humility remain critical if leaders are to transcend their pitfalls and foster a culture of collaboration, innovation, and sustained success in their organizations.

Voices of Dissent

In the corridors of corporate power, where decisions ripple outward like waves in a pond, the voices of dissent often struggle to rise above the cacophony of arrogance. These voices—those of employees, team members, and even junior leaders—represent the pulse of an organization. Yet they can be silenced, muffled by the prideful demeanor of leaders who perceive dissent as a threat rather than an opportunity for growth.

The stories that follow shine a light on the real-life experiences of individuals who dared to express their concerns to leaders entrenched in their own perceptions of infallibility. It is in these narratives that the profound impact of prideful leadership on team morale can be observed, revealing the intrinsic need for an open dialogue between those at the helm and those following in their wake.

Emma was a marketing manager in a prominent tech company, her trajectory marked by dedication and spirited innovation. Known for her creativity and tenacity, she had a knack for delivering results that surpassed expectations. However, a shift in leadership brought with it a new director, Alan, whose reputation for success came with equally steep tales of dismissiveness towards feedback. Alan's approach, though initially refreshing, quickly morphed into a prideful fortress, where dissenting opinions were met with disdain.

On one occasion, Emma uncovered troubling data from a recent campaign that contradicted Alan's narrative of unmitigated success. Armed with numbers and insights, she approached Alan, hoping for a constructive discussion. Instead, she encountered a fortress of arrogance that reeked of entitlement. "I appreciate your enthusiasm, Emma, but I assure you, you're misinterpreting the data. Our results speak for themselves."

Feeling invisible, Emma recalled how pride had turned Alan from an inspiring leader into an immovable gargoyle. "The moment I sensed his dismissiveness, I knew I had to tread lightly. The pressure to conform stifled any creativity I once had. I wasn't just unhappy; I felt that my voice was actively unwelcome."

Emma's struggle was not unique. Across various organizations and industries, stories echo similar sentiments. Joe, a junior software developer, found himself in a similar predicament with his project manager, Sarah. Tasked with implementing new software features, Joe had reservations about deadlines that seemed unrealistic, but each time he raised his concerns, Sarah's demeanor shifted. Her pride, fortified by past successes, left little room for dialogue.

"It felt as if I were talking to a wall," Joe recalled. "Every time I mentioned my fears about the deadline, she would brush it off. She'd smile and say, 'Trust the plan,' but the more she dismissed my opinions, the more I realized she didn't care about team insight; she just wanted to showcase a perfect product based on her timeline."

The impact of Sarah's arrogance was pervasive. Team morale plummeted as Joe's colleagues observed the futility of their efforts to introduce healthy debate in meetings. The shared anxiety became an undercurrent that poisoned collaboration. Tasks were rushed, errors unfolded, and frustration grew until the team reached a boiling point when a critical flaw in the software caused a significant setback.

Reflecting on that shift, Joe remarked, "We could have avoided that failure if Sarah had just been open to our feedback. We knew where the pitfalls lay, but our voices were silenced. It's heartbreaking to see a good team unravel solely because of a leader's pride."

Regrettably, the tendency for leaders to bask in their own reflections fundamentally alters the landscape of communication within an organization. Employees often weigh the risks of voicing dissent against the potential fallout from a leader resistant to feedback. While the desire for harmony within a team is natural, it becomes a breeding ground for toxicity when leaders misinterpret it as an endorsement of their arrogance.

As voices subside, a singular narrative prevails, reinforcing the cycle of complacency. It becomes difficult, if not impossible, for individuals to feel valued. A survey conducted by a respected consultancy firm found that nearly 65% of employees reported hesitance in voicing concerns for fear of repercussions. The statistic alone is a sobering testament to the hazards posed when pride morphs into arrogance.

To illustrate this further, the experience of Lena, a project coordinator in healthcare, offers a compelling lens. Overcomplicated project timelines devised by her manager, Tom, began to set the stage for turmoil. Lena and her team identified various risks to patient safety stemming from rushed implementations, but any attempt to communicate this was met with Tom's resolute arrogance.

"He would say, 'We've done it this way before and it worked, so stop worrying.' It felt like he wanted us to adopt his attitude rather than focus on the outcomes we were responsible for. I was frustrated but also terrified of pushing back. How do you challenge a leader who projects unshakeable confidence?" Lena recounted.

Tom's pride resulted not only in a lack of trust in team insights but also in a deteriorating team culture. As the pressure mounted, Lena began to notice the emotional toll on her colleagues. Those who had once been driven and enthusiastic became withdrawn, burying feelings of insecurity and discontent. The fear of conflict overshadowed their ambitions, leading them to silence rather than voice dissent—even when patient safety was at stake.

During one particularly intense meeting, Lena decided to raise her concerns, albeit hesitantly. As she spoke, she could see Tom's expression harden. The air grew thick with tension, and she pivoted quickly, realizing she'd breached an invisible barrier.

Subsequently, Tom's response was dismissive and condescending: "I would think you of all people would trust the decisions I make for this team. You don't want to look unprofessional, do you?" The backhanded remark shattered Lena's confidence, echoing in the minds of her colleagues. In a twisted game of power, Tom subordinated dissent under pride, firmly entrenching himself behind an insurmountable façade of leadership.

The cost of such invisibility is often felt in the very foundations of organizations. High turnover rates, disengaged employees, and a lack of innovation are dismal outcomes that arise from team members feeling unheard. The narrative does not merely belong to the disgruntled voices; it reveals a significant organizational pattern of disengagement. Companies that embrace open communication thrive, while those that suppress dissent find themselves in a regression of innovation and productivity.

The repercussions of arrogant leadership become even more evident when contrasting the experiences of those who have successfully navigated similar dilemmas with leaders who prioritize collaboration over a rigid hierarchy. In a tech start-up named InnovateX, the CEO, Marcus, displayed an appreciation for feedback that empowered rather than stifled his employees.

Marcus was often characterized by his humility and willingness to accept shortcomings. His leadership approach involved soliciting dissenting views and encouraging open debate. One particular instance stands out, where a developer, Zara, had raised concerns about an impending product deadline that could compromise the company's quality standards.

Instead of dismissing Zara's concerns, Marcus actively invited further discussion. "It's not just about meeting the deadline; it's about ensuring we deliver value to our users, too. Let's gather everyone's insights and explore how we can address this together," Marcus encouraged.

The shift in atmosphere was palpable. Zara felt empowered, and her team willingly engaged in open discussions that highlighted potential consequences more effectively than any solitary voice could summon. With all perspectives gathered, they collaborated to create a roadmap that balanced ethics with deadlines—a feat unachievable under a leader inclined to foster pride over collaboration.

The contrast between Marcus and leaders like Alan, Sarah, and Tom is stark. In Marcus's case, an open approach nurtures a culture of trust, where dissent transforms from a perceived threat into a catalyst for creativity and innovation. Employees who felt free to express their opinions dispelled the fog of complacency while improving relationships. This cultural ethos not only benefitted individual morale but also translated into robust organizational performance—demonstrating that receptiveness to feedback is intrinsic to sustainable success.

Comparative narratives from Emma, Joe, Lena, and their peers serve as cautionary tales. Teams thrive under leaders who acknowledge the significance of every voice and remain approachable, encouraging discussions that challenge the status quo. The stories highlight that pride can indeed be a double-edged sword; when wielded with wisdom, it inspires confidence. However, when it turns toward arrogance, it endangers the bonds of trust that knit effective teams together.

It is essential for leaders to recognize that arrogance can mask the vulnerabilities that inherently accompany leadership roles. When leaders dismiss feedback due to pride, they accumulate a dangerous reservoir of discontent that can act like a ticking time bomb—innocuous at first but destructive when detonated. The lesson here is not merely about the need for leaders to become aware of dissent; it's about fostering a culture that welcomes it.

Organizations must actively cultivate in their leadership the principle that dissent isn't synonymous with disloyalty. Employees should feel encouraged to express their thoughts freely, knowing that their feedback might just ignite a solution that propels the organization forward. As leaders adapt their mindsets from defensive arrogance to an embrace of humility, they set the stage for collaboration to flourish.

As we draw upon the rich tapestry of experiences shared by various employees in response to prideful leaders, it becomes clear that the path to true leadership lies not solely in self-assurance but in the courage to listen, to learn, and to adapt. The power of dissent is profound; it wears the garb of loyalty, dressing itself in perspectives meant to inform and enhance, not diminish. Leaders who acknowledge this power can transform their teams not just from within but as part of the broader organizational fabric.

In essence, embracing dissent can lead to profound organizational growth, creating harmonies of collaboration, engagement, and innovation. As we reflect on these narratives of voicing dissent, let them serve as reminders of the necessity to cultivate an environment where feedback is celebrated rather than suppressed, nurturing the pathways to sustainable success.

Balancing Confidence and Humility

In today's rapidly evolving landscape of leadership, the dichotomy of confidence and humility can often create a complex interplay that defines a leader's effectiveness. Many leaders grapple with the fine line between being self-assured and tipping over into arrogance. The transformational journey of leadership requires not only understanding these concepts but also implementing strategies that create a sustainable balance between them.

Confidence, when harnessed positively, breeds the kind of audacity necessary for leaders to take risks that can propel their organizations forward. Humility, on the other hand, remains a cornerstone of authentic leadership, promoting a collaborative environment where team members feel valued and empowered. Therefore, cultivating a culture where pride manifests as confidence and is tempered by humility is essential for effective leadership.

One of the key strategies we will explore in this subchapter is the practice of intentional vulnerability. Leaders who demonstrate vulnerability foster an authentic environment where others feel safe to express their ideas, concerns, and challenges. This transparency not only strengthens relationships but also encourages accountability and growth.

Intentional vulnerability does not mean revealing every flaw or mistake; rather, it is about acknowledging one's limitations and asking for help when necessary. This approach allows leaders to showcase their humanity, making it easier for others to connect with them. For example, a leader facing a challenging decision might consult their team, inviting them to share their insights and expertise. This not only cultivates trust but signals that the leader values collective wisdom over individual bravado.

However, vulnerability alone is insufficient without a firm foundation rooted in self-awareness. Leaders must possess an acute understanding of their strengths and weaknesses. The practice of self-reflection can be invaluable in this regard. Regularly evaluating one's actions, decisions, and communication styles can illuminate areas where confidence may be veering toward arrogance.

To aid in self-awareness, leaders can adopt techniques such as journaling or soliciting feedback from peers and team members. Constructive criticism should be embraced as a tool for growth rather than a threat to one's authority. By modeling this behavior, leaders create a culture where feedback is normalized, making it a vital part of organizational dynamics.

Additionally, implementing regular performance reviews that emphasize both achievements and areas for improvement can foster a growth mindset within the team. Leaders should also encourage their teams to engage in self-assessment, reinforcing the idea that everyone has the capacity for growth. This collective journey in self-discovery nourishes an environment where humility celebrates progress, curbing the risk of arrogance.

Next, we delve into the concept of mentorship as another pivotal strategy to maintain balance. Mentorship, whether formal or informal, can provide critical insight into the subtleties of confidence and humility. Seasoned leaders can offer guidance on how to navigate complex situations and make difficult decisions while remaining grounded.

Emerging leaders benefit tremendously from the wisdom of their more experienced counterparts. A mentoring dynamic allows for open dialogue about successes and failures, bridging the gap between confidence and humility. When leaders have mentors who model humility, it encourages them to adopt similar traits in their own leadership practice. This relationship fosters a continuous learning culture that inherently supports the growth of both confidence and humility.

Moreover, organizations should strive to create systems that celebrate not only individual successes but also teamwork. A culture of collaboration underscores the notion that while confidence is essential, collective achievements are what truly drive progress. Recognizing the contributions of each team member not only mitigates the risk of individual ego but also highlights the importance of humility within the collective.

In this vein, leaders must also be vigilant against the dangers of ego-driven achievements. When leaders highlight their accomplishments at the expense of their team's contributions, it sets a precedent that may lead to a toxic atmosphere. Instead, utilizing language that emphasizes collaborative efforts—such as 'we' instead of 'I'—promotes humility and recognizes the value of the team.

Another strategy for balancing confidence with humility lies in the pursuit of continuous learning. Leaders should position themselves as lifelong learners, actively seeking opportunities for professional development. Investing time in workshops, seminars, or online courses not only broadens a leader's knowledge base but reinforces the idea that no one knows everything.

This commitment to learning can take several forms. For instance, leaders can participate in cross-functional trainings that provide insight into other departments. This not only enhances their understanding of the organization but also fosters empathy towards team members across various roles. Furthermore, sharing their learning experiences with the team demonstrates a commitment to growth and invites others to embark on their learning journeys.

Additionally, leaders can invite guest speakers or industry experts to share their insights, presenting a wealth of knowledge that further instills the value of humility. This can allow teams to benefit from external perspectives while encouraging dialogue around learning rather than competition.

Creating space for failure is another critical aspect of fostering humility amid confidence. It is imperative to acknowledge that failure is a natural part of growth. Leaders should normalize discussions around failures, treating them as educational experiences. When leaders candidly share their setbacks, it reinforces the idea that mistakes are not fatal but rather valuable lessons from which to derive insights.

John, a CEO of a tech startup, made headlines when he openly discussed how a failed product launch had forced his company to reevaluate its direction. By sharing the missteps leading up to the launch, he not only maintained his team's confidence but also cultivated a culture where experimentation is embraced. His team felt empowered to voice their ideas and take risks, understanding that failures would be met with support rather than blame.

Moreover, celebrating diverse viewpoints within the organization is another strategy to balance confidence and humility. Leaders should encourage team members to express their perspectives, irrespective of their hierarchical standing. In practice, this means creating forums where employees feel secure in sharing their ideas. By valuing contributions from everyone, leaders demonstrate that while confidence in their judgment is important, the voices of the collective hold immense value as well.

To operationalize this approach, leaders might implement regular brainstorming sessions and encourage input from various levels within the organization. It could be as simple as an open-door policy, or structured like an 'idea box' where team members can submit suggestions anonymously. When innovative ideas arise, successful leaders make it a point to credit the originating source, thereby reinforcing the cultural norms of humility and appreciation.

Lastly, leveraging storytelling as a tool can significantly impact how leaders embody and demonstrate the balance between confidence and humility. Personal anecdotes recounted by leaders can serve as powerful lessons for their teams. These stories often resonate more deeply than abstract principles, providing relatable illustrations of lessons learned through experience.

Narratives that encompass both triumphs and challenges paint a holistic picture of what it means to lead. By sharing these experiences of overcoming obstacles while remaining grounded, leaders instill confidence in their teams while also modeling the importance of humility. It inspires employees to develop their own stories rooted in growth, courage, and resilience.

In conclusion, creating a balanced environment where confidence does not stray into arrogance requires intentionality and effort from leaders. By fostering intentional vulnerability, cultivating self-awareness, implementing mentorship programs, promoting continuous learning, normalizing discussions around failure, honoring diverse viewpoints, and utilizing storytelling, leaders can pave the way for a culture that values both confidence and humility.

As we navigate the complexities of leadership in a rapidly changing world, the dialogue surrounding pride and its manifestations will inevitably evolve. However, the foundational elements of relationship-building through balance will remain vital as leaders strive for authenticity in their practice. The synergy formed from this balance not only invigorates organizational culture but ultimately drives sustainable success through shared values anchored in respect, trust, and collaboration.

THE DANGERS OF COMPLACENCY

The Illusion of Stability

Complacency often lulls organizations into a false sense of security. Like a serene lake—a beautiful façade concealing turbulent currents just beneath the surface—it can create an illusion of stability that grows increasingly deceptive over time. Leaders may believe everything is running smoothly, unaware that beneath the placid surface, challenges and changes are brewing, waiting for the right moment to surface and create chaos. This metaphor serves as a lens through which we can explore the dangers of complacency, examining how organizations that fall into a comfort zone are prone to missed opportunities, stagnation, and ultimately, decline.

Consider the story of Axiom Corporation, once a leading player in the tech industry, known for its groundbreaking innovations and market leadership. In its prime, Axiom thrived on creativity, pushing boundaries, and setting trends. However, as the market matured and competition intensified, the company's leadership began to feel a sense of comfort in its established position. The team began to underestimate the significance of emerging competitors and shifting consumer preferences, casting aside their once-vibrant culture of innovation.

Gradually, the boards of directors found themselves in meetings characterized by easy consensus rather than vigorous debates. The CEO, once an emblem of vision and ambition, began prioritizing maintaining stability over pursuing risk-taking ventures. A culture of complacency took root, and the organization's spirit of challenge dulled.

Years later, when a new competitor named Innovent burst onto the scene with disruptive technologies and agile methodologies, Axiom struggled to respond. The slip between complacency and actual instability was so subtle; the leadership team believed they were still on firm ground, unaware of the extent to which their market relevance had eroded. They were met with dismal sales figures, declining market shares, and an increasingly demoralized workforce. It was a wake-up call punctuated by layoffs and lost projects.

Reflecting on that experience, Axiom's former CEO, Miriam Patel, noted, "We were like a beautiful lake, so calm on the surface. But as the currents began to shift, we struggled to stay afloat because we hadn't realized what was going on below. We took our position for granted and fell victim to our own success."

The story of Axiom Corp serves as a stark reminder of how easily stability can breed complacency. Leaders, in their quest to preserve what is working, may inadvertently stifle the very innovation that initially propelled them forward. They fail to recognize that comfort breeds stagnation, and stagnation inevitably leads to decline.

The illusion of stability often manifests in various forms, not just at an organizational level but also within teams and individual leadership styles. For instance, a confident leader may stop seeking input from team members after a string of successful projects. This withdrawal from active engagement fosters complacency among team members who may grow indifferent to the evolving landscape of their industry. Collaboration wanes, and innovative strategies fall by the wayside.

This complacency also permeates the corporate culture. As teams become less willing to take risks or voice dissent, innovative thinking is discouraged. Employees may fear rocking the boat, leading to an environment where groupthink predominates, further shielding the organization from necessary change. A culture that once thrived on challenge now finds itself trapped in an echo chamber, reinforcing outdated ideas and practices.

Consider another vivid illustration: the case of Harmony Health Systems. This organization had long championed patient-centric care and won several accolades for its innovative health initiatives. However, over time, the leadership focused on maintaining their reputation within existing frameworks rather than exploring new, disruptive opportunities in the rapidly evolving healthcare landscape. Leadership believed that their established methods were sufficient, and began evading discussions about emerging technologies like telehealth, which their patients were increasingly seeking.

Leadership's insistence on holding onto their tried-and-true methods ultimately bred an environment where complacency thrived. Frontline staff reported feeling unheard, and many left their positions in search of environments that valued innovation and adaptability. As a result, Harmony Health Systems not only began to lose its reputation as a trailblazer but also faced substantial financial pressure when competitors surged ahead with novel approaches that attracted patients.

Dr. Ethan Grant, a former executive at Harmony, reflected on the organization's plight: "Looking back, it's clear we became enamored with our stability and our past successes. We had strong leaders at the helm, but their unwillingness to question our approach became our downfall. It was as if we were floating on the lake, oblivious to the changes stirring beneath."

The continued exploration of how complacency manifests can also uncover uncomfortable truths about how organizations measure success. Traditional metrics that focus on profitability, market share, or customer satisfaction can contribute to a stagnant mindset, fostering an environment resistant to change. Instead of probing deeper, leaders often celebrate short-term gains, weakening their organizational resilience in the long run.

When external pressures arise—such as technological advancements, regulatory changes, or shifts in consumer behavior—complacent organizations may find themselves struggling to pivot or adapt. The initial signs of a shifting tide may be ignored, leading to an eventual reckoning when those tides can no longer be held back. Consider the automotive industry, where companies like General Motors once dominated but faced existential challenges from nimble competitors such as Tesla that prioritized innovation over past successes.

The complacency that pervaded GM's leadership for years is apparent in hindsight. With the recognition of electric vehicles on the horizon, they lethargically pursued incremental improvements instead of laser-focusing on emerging technologies. "It was an internal struggle between embracing new pathways or clinging to old hopes of sustaining a once-great legacy," reflected former GM executive Linda Tran. "We latterly recognized that the currents were shifting, yet we were still floating on that serene surface, certain our way was still the right way. But we faced the harsh reality once we began to sink."

Given these cautionary tales, it's essential for leaders to confront their own complacency and elicit a culture of constant vigilance and openness. However, recognizing and addressing complacency within an organization can feel daunting. Many leaders struggle to provoke healthy conflict, fearing it may shatter the much-desired tranquility, leading to defensive reactions and disengagement.

Nevertheless, fostering a culture of accountability will reinvigorate conversations around growth and innovation. Leaders should implement programs and structures that encourage team members to voice concerns and constructively challenge the status quo without fear of retaliation. By creating channels for open dialogue, leaders can turn discontent into a rich tapestry of diverse thoughts that challenge complacency.

The transformative impact of transformative practices is evidenced in organizations that choose to lead with vulnerability and promote collective ownership. They remain committed to continual learning, fueled by a steadfast belief that every setback serves as a valuable teaching moment. This commitment to growth allows organizations to embrace change proactively, creating strategic responses that foster collaboration and communication.

Resilience in leadership is often about accepting the unpredictable nature of existence while remaining grounded in actionable principles. Leaders can harness the chaos inherent in change by developing and nurturing a shared set of values that drive their teams toward a unified purpose. This cognizance invites diverse perspectives, leading to innovative solutions instead of entrenched complacency.

For many organizations, the first step is conducting a thorough self-assessment to identify triggers of complacency. A holistic evaluation will reveal patterns of behavior that undermine progress. As part of this assessment, gathering real-time employee feedback will highlight underlying issues often masked by surface-level success. This feedback can often uncover areas ripe for improvement, reframing perspectives that transcend the individual departments or silos that often compartmentalize organizations.

Moreover, leaders should contextualize challenges wrought by complacency within team storytelling—creating narratives that connect team members, enlightening them about past lessons while inspiring imminent action. Shared stories can empower leaders to frame their collective experiences and imbue teams with a sense of ownership over their engagement with their work culture and organizational mission.

As organizations implement changes that reflect an understanding of their complacency, the question arises as to how leaders should measure their success moving forward. Traditionally employed metrics can often mislead, encouraging leaders to assess progress solely based on tangible outcomes. However, including qualitative measures can mitigate this misperception of performance by ensuring conversations remain dynamic.

Leaders might choose to implement structured yet adaptive feedback mechanisms that not only consider short-term metrics but also long-term impacts on the organization's culture, innovation capacity, and employee engagement levels. By encouraging continuous feedback loops, outreach accountability initiatives can keep teams aligned and agile as they progress through both challenges and successes.

Ultimately, the task of overcoming complacency lies in leaders' hands, demanding courage, honesty, and foresight. Organizations that manage complacency successfully become akin to tuned instruments that harmonize collective efforts, resonating innovative ideas, and moving toward shared ambitions. In fostering a culture that celebrates growth over complacency, leaders become active agents of change, steering their teams safely through even the most turbulent waters.

One of the clearest answers to the illusion of stability is that leadership must remain as dynamic and flexible as the world around them. As leaders embark on their journeys free from complacency, they reflect an essential truth: while lakes can appear serene, the currents below can shift unexpectedly. It is within these shifts that leaders must thrive, cultivating both awareness and agility that move beyond the tranquility of complacency, navigating toward a future teeming with opportunities.

Strategizing Against Complacency

In any organization, complacency can become an insidious presence, creeping in when leaders and teams become overly comfortable with the status quo. As history has shown, even the most prosperous organizations can succumb to stagnation due to complacency, losing their competitive edge and jeopardizing their long-term viability. To combat this pervasive threat, leaders must adopt strategic frameworks that actively foster a culture of engagement, continuous learning, and innovation. This subchapter aims to provide practical methods to help leaders set the stage for transformative growth by actively combating complacency through reflective practices, regular check-ins on team morale, and innovation initiatives.

The first step in strategizing against complacency is establishing a culture of reflective practice. Reflection is a powerful tool for leaders; it encourages thoughtful analysis of past actions, decisions, and outcomes. When leaders engage in reflective practice, they are better equipped to recognize patterns of complacency that might be festering within the organization. One effective way to embed reflection into the organizational culture is to dedicate time for leaders and teams to review their successes and failures regularly.

Setting aside specific times for reflection can take many forms. For instance, organizations might implement weekly or monthly reflection sessions where teams are encouraged to discuss the following:

1. **Achievements and Setbacks:** Team members should share their successes and challenges openly, allowing for collaborative problem-solving and learning opportunities. By discussing both achievements and setbacks, teams cultivate a growth mindset that embraces the notion that every experience contributes to development.

2. **Learning from Each Other:** Encouraging partnerships and open discussions can lead to unique insights from diverse perspectives within the team. Peer feedback sessions are instrumental in offering insights that can spark innovative ideas or highlight areas of improvement, thus preventing stagnation.

3. **Evaluating Goals:** Regularly evaluating organizational goals against team performance can help identify areas where complacency might have taken hold. If a team is not progressing toward its objectives, reflective practices can expose underlying reasons and enable leaders to recalibrate their strategies accordingly.

Moreover, leaders must model the practice of reflection themselves to create a ripple effect throughout the organization. By openly discussing their own reflections, leaders inspire an environment where team members feel safe to express thoughts and ideas, fostering transparency and vulnerability.

Another critical method for combating complacency is conducting regular check-ins on team morale. These check-ins serve as a temperature gauge for the organization, allowing leaders to identify and address potential issues before they escalate. High morale indicates that a team is engaged, productive, and motivated, while low morale can signal a brewing complacency problem.

To make check-ins effective, leaders can adopt the following strategies:

1. **One-on-One Meetings:** Schedule regular individual check-ins with team members. These meetings create a safe space for employees to share their thoughts and feelings about their roles, workloads, and team dynamics. It also allows leaders to garner individual insights that may be masked in larger group settings. Additionally, these meetings convey to employees that their voices are valued, promoting a culture of trust and

openness.

2. **Anonymous Surveys:** Implementing anonymous team surveys can offer deeper insights into team morale without the fears of repercussions. This method encourages candid feedback regarding workplace dynamics, engagement, and satisfaction. The data collected from these surveys should be analyzed carefully, with actionable steps derived from the results to develop plans addressing any identified issues.

3. **Interactive Team Workshops:** Facilitating workshops that encourage team members to express their thoughts on company culture and workflows can provide rich feedback on morale. These environments foster honest dialogue and can surface complacency issues that may not be evident to leadership.

As a leader, being proactive about addressing morale signals a commitment to maintaining a positive and engaged workplace. By making the well-being of their teams a priority, leaders establish rapport and loyalty, which, in turn, minimize complacency.

Navigating through a complacent environment requires innovation initiatives that can energize teams and inspire change. Developing a culture of innovation is vital in keeping leadership agile and engaged while also actively combatting complacency. Here are some effective initiatives to promote innovation throughout the organization:

1. **Innovation Labs:** Creating dedicated spaces for experimentation allows team members to brainstorm, prototype, and test new ideas outside of their day-to-day responsibilities. These labs can foster collaboration across departments and provide an opportunity for staff to explore innovative solutions without the constraints of their primary job functions.

2. **Encouraging risk-taking:** Establishing organizational policies that reward creativity and calculated risk-taking can help shift the culture from one that fears failure to one that embraces the opportunities for learning that come from experimentation. Leaders should ifneeded share stories of failure alongside success, illustrating that not every idea will bear fruit — and that's okay.

3. **Hackathons:** Hosting time-limited hackathons or innovation challenges can mobilize team members around specific organizational problems or goals. These events foster enthusiasm and collaboration, allowing participants to share ideas, ultimately leading to breakthrough innovations. This energetic environment, where everyone is focused on problem-solving, can invigorate teams and foster a collective sense of purpose.

4. **Cross-functional Teams:** Encouraging collaboration across different functional areas allows for a blending of ideas and expertise. Forming cross-functional teams for specific projects can help break down silos, stimulating creative thinking amongst diverse skill sets. By bringing diverse minds together, leaders can generate innovative solutions that may have remained dormant within a complacent environment.

5. **Continuous Learning Opportunities:** Providing ongoing training and professional development for team members cultivates a culture of growth. Leaders should prioritize offering workshops, seminars, and resources that challenge their employees to expand their knowledge and skills. This focus on continuous development demonstrates a commitment to adaptability, further countering complacency.

In summary, strategizing against complacency involves a multifaceted approach that engages leaders and team members alike. Reflective practices, regular morale check-ins, and innovation initiatives serve as powerful tools in dismantling complacency within organizations.

To successfully implement these strategies, leaders must:

- **Foster Trust:** Create a safe environment that encourages open communication, collaboration, and generous sharing of insights. The more secure team members feel, the more likely they are to express their thoughts and participate in reflective and innovative practices.

- **Encourage Autonomy:** Empower employees by granting them the authority to take ownership of their work and explore innovative solutions. Empowerment facilitates a sense of accountability, helping to combat the disengagement associated with complacent environments.

- **Lead by Example:** Leaders themselves must embody these strategies, demonstrating commitment to reflection, morale evaluation, and innovation. Their genuine enthusiasm for combating complacency will inspire similar behaviors in their teams.

Tackling complacency is an ongoing process requiring intention and diligence. As leaders become vigilant in recognizing complacent behaviors and fostering an environment of continuous growth, they lay the groundwork for an organization that remains dynamic, innovative, and agile. In this way, leaders set themselves up not only for current success but for sustainable achievement in future endeavors.

The Ripple Effect of Inaction

In a vast and serene lake, the surface appears calm and inviting, a perfect reflection of the blue sky above. To the untrained eye, it may seem as if everything is in order under its placid veneer. However, look closer, and you'll find the depths stirred with unseen currents, hidden turbulence that can disrupt the surface calm. This metaphor paints the picture of how complacency in an organization operates. Though it may seem stable and secure, beneath the surface lies a myriad of issues that can cause a significant upheaval, sending shockwaves through every level of the organization. The ripple effect of inaction, often masked by superficial tranquility, can have far-reaching consequences that undermine both morale and productivity.

Complacency often sneaks into organizations under the guise of stability. When trends appear to be favorable, and the competition seems distant, leadership can grow comfortable, prioritizing routine maintenance over dynamic engagement. Employees may feel encouraged to coast along, riding out the momentum built by previous successes. However, once the tide of change begins to roll in, that previous comfort can quickly become a sinking ship. It is here that complacency's true danger surfaces, influencing behaviors, cultures, and ultimately, performance.

Take, for example, the case of a medium-sized tech firm, NeuroTech Solutions. For years, NeuroTech was a shining star in the software development space, producing innovative applications that garnered accolades and revenue equally. Their CEO, a charismatic leader, built a culture based on enthusiasm and creativity during the company's initial growth phases. Growth led to a robust team filled with talent and ambition. However, as the company gained market share, the leadership team began to rest on their laurels, trusting that their past achievements would secure their future. The quest for innovation became stale; meetings became perfunctory, and the once-vibrant discussions fell silent.

As months rolled by, employees started recognizing a stark disconnect between the leadership's complacency and the emerging industry disruptions. They saw new competitors innovating at an unprecedented pace while NeuroTech clung to outdated practices and ideas. With each passing day, team morale plummeted. Employees no longer felt their voices mattered; instead, they felt confined to a stifling routine that inhibited creativity. Those who once had a passion for their projects lost their drive, viewing work as merely a paycheck rather than a vehicle for progress.

In boardrooms filled with silence, where once laughter and brainstorming echoed, leadership began wondering why project deadlines were missed and why employees seemed disengaged. The initial reaction was bewilderment, followed by confusion that turned to frustration. The disconnect opened a chasm between leadership and employees, a precipice that few sought to navigate. When leaders chose to turn a blind eye to the creeping malaise that permeated the organization, employees began to withdraw further into themselves. They ceased sharing their innovative ideas, their feedback silenced by an environment that no longer celebrated dissent or discussion. This spiraled into a tactical paralysis, where, inaction became the norm, amplifying feelings of hopelessness and dissatisfaction.

One well-respected engineer at NeuroTech, Olivia, found herself in this predicament. With a track record of successful projects, Olivia was passionate about incorporating groundbreaking concepts into application design. However, as she presented new ideas in meetings, she was met with blank stares, disinterest, or, worse, outright dismissal.

Frustrated with the inaction and the overwhelming atmosphere of complacency, Olivia eventually chose to limit her participation. She resigned herself to completing her tasks without attempting to innovate or inspire. Many employees followed suit, leading to a work environment characterized by a lack of enthusiasm. They exchanged innovation for monotony, allowing the lake's surface to remain eerily still while rapid currents churned beneath.

To further illustrate this point, let's delve into a retail company, BrightGoods, which experienced its downfall due to resting on its laurels. With a robust lineup of seasonal products, BrightGoods thrived in the community, becoming a favorite local shopping destination. Employees thrilled at the energy surrounding marketing campaigns, and customers flocked to stores. Year after year, the company maintained profitability, and leadership felt justified in their repetitive strategy, assuming that past success predicted future performance.

However, as e-commerce exploded, BrightGoods further alienated itself from its clientele who began to demand better online shopping experiences. Competition emerged swiftly, disrupting previously stable market positions. BrightGoods leadership chose to dismiss initial marketplace changes, labeling them as passing trends. Instead of adapting to detail, leadership stuck to traditional practices—weekly sales, ads in local newspapers, and clearance events during the holidays.

Gradually, employees noticed an influx of dissatisfied customers seeking convenience, ease of access, and a dynamic shopping experience. Unable to understand leadership's reluctance to evolve, the workforce became frustrated. Sales associates, instead of providing solutions, often found themselves apologizing for the limited product selection and outdated website features. This rife dissatisfaction led workers to disengage, undermining service quality and, subsequently, customer experience. The ripple effect impacted not just employee morale but also stung the brand image, cutting into sales as patrons flocked to competitors who adapted more quickly.

As BrightGoods faced increasing losses in revenue, its leadership convened urgently. They looked for answers as to why their attempts to revive sales strategies fell flat. Blind to the root cause of their crisis, they emphasized restructuring sales approaches—open talks surrounding feedback were dismissed, leaving staff bewildered. Employees felt as though their insights and perspectives led to little more than silent exchanges, reinforcing the grip of complacency throughout the organization.

Universally, the patterns reveal an unfortunate truth; complacency breeds inaction, leading to destructive ripple effects rippling out in waves. It is easy for leaders to assume that a lack of visible issues signifies a healthy organization. However, beneath a calm exterior awaits an undercurrent of concerns capable of destabilizing an entire company. Those patterns share one telling commonality: when leadership fails to engage proactively with its teams and address encroaching complacency, they risk losing talent, morale, and, ultimately, their competitive edge.

It becomes imperative, therefore, for leaders to recognize this malaise and act on its cues visibly. Engaging employees actively is crucial in building a culture of accountability that pushes back against complacency. When leaders embrace feedback and are willing to adapt, they create an environment where employees feel inspired and challenged, breaking away from comfort zones.

Let's go back to Olivia at NeuroTech. An inspiring shift occurred when a new CTO was appointed amid the company's stagnancy. Unlike previous leadership, this new leader focused on fostering dialogue and setting constructive discussions into play. The dynamic instigated a series of town hall meetings and brainstorming sessions, working to cultivate a pathway that re-engaged the workforce. Employees watched, hopeful; could possible revitalization take place? As lines of communication opened, conversations that had long since ceased sprang back to life.

Olivia, too, felt the tide shifting. New policies emphasized feedback and empathetic leadership. With the opportunity to voice her ideas and feel heard, she began participating in discussions, reigniting the passion she once had for her work. The once-stagnant lake began to ripple with currents of innovation, leaving behind the tranquil facade once thought indestructible. Employees collaborated with newfound energy, allowing them to test ideas and share perceived industry shifts, appreciating a culture that valued dissent.

On the other end of the spectrum, let's now turn to the successive events at BrightGoods. Instead of reflecting post-crisis, the leadership aimed to hastily implement drastic changes without engaging the employees who had repeatedly voiced concerns during meetings. An internal audit appeared, yet with no opportunities for staff input, the initiatives described merely mirrored adjustments without apparent acknowledgment of underlying issues. Employees quickly reverted to their disengaged state, recognizing that their experiences and insights remained dismissed and out of view.

As the trade-offs unfolded, disengagement strengthened its hold in the workplace; exceptional employees sought opportunities elsewhere, and customer feedback continued to dwindle. The spiral ensued, showcasing the ripple effect: from leadership inaction to employee discontent, essentially diminishing brand presence and health. The leaders missed vital opportunities to engage within their ranks, choosing complacency instead of pursuing constructive conversations that could have arguably transformed their outlook. Altogether, stagnation asserted itself as an inescapable trend, encapsulating the gravity of a company stuck in on its past.

The consequences of complacency reverberate well beyond what meets the eye, reinforcing the importance of leaders addressing culture head-on. Real stories highlight this experience, weaving together themes of accountability and engagement that emerging leaders must embrace. Organizations that imbue leadership with humility and transparency thrive in reframing setbacks and learning from them.

In turn, the antidote to this complacency lies in proactive leadership that opens themselves to vulnerability. Rather than merely waiting for insights to surface, leaders must always take the pulse of the organization by examining engagement metrics, sentiments, and ultimately sustaining dialogical spaces for reflection.

Feedback loops and assessments are vital to avoid the traps of inaction. They create opportunities to measure how employees feel, encouraging direct lines for insight into their experiences. Additionally, fostering a culture of courage encourages workers to voice observations when complacency emerges, ensuring these voices are treated with genuine respect rather than mere acknowledgment. During this engagement process, leadership models an environment that values proactivity and mutual accountability, establishing collective progress built on transparency.

Understanding the ripple effects of inaction emphasizes one critical lesson: leadership accountability is the cornerstone of organizational health. Leaders today must tread lightly on complacency's treacherous ground, empowering their teams through open discussion, transparent practices, and nourishing feedback that fosters continual growth. By doing so, they motivate momentum and prevent complacency from taking root within their organization, causing waves of decay that could contribute not just to stagnation but systemic ruin.

The myth of the calm lake must be dismantled; complacency thrives in the silence that follows inaction. As leaders understand the need for proactive engagement, they begin to surface conversations that shine a light on critical issues, ushering in a culture where accountability reigns supreme. The ripple effect, rather than a path to ruin, transitions to an expansive network of collaboration, insight, and thriving organizational health.

CHAPTER FIVE

HARNESSING CONFLICT AS AN ALLY

The Power of Constructive Conflict

Conflict is often seen in a negative light, a disruption to harmony that leaders should work tirelessly to avoid. However, this perspective fails to recognize the profound potential that constructive conflict possesses. When harnessed effectively, conflict can act as a catalyst for growth, an engine that drives innovation, and a tool for building stronger, more resilient teams. This subchapter emphasizes the transformational power of conflict when approached with courage, recounting powerful examples of teams that flourished after facing challenges head-on, showcasing how dissent often leads to innovative solutions and fosters a culture of collaboration.

Let's set the stage with a powerful example from the tech industry. When Google was developing its first iteration of Gmail, the project faced numerous internal challenges. Engineers disagreed on the fundamental architecture of the system. Some believed that a traditional approach would suffice; others championed a more radical, innovative design that could scale with their growing user base. They were at an impasse, as both sides were firmly convinced they held the best solution.

Rather than sweeping the disagreement under the rug or encouraging a false sense of harmony, project leaders decided to embrace the conflict. They organized a series of workshops where each faction could present their ideas and the rationale behind them. The sessions were intense, featuring heated debates and spirited discussions. Team members were encouraged to push back, question assumptions, and propose alternative ideas.

As these sessions played out, a remarkable evolution took place. The engineers began to understand each other's perspectives. They recognized the strengths and weaknesses of each approach and began to see how their ideas could complement rather than contradict one another. Through this constructive conflict, the project team ultimately developed a hybrid solution that combined the best elements of both architectural strategies, leading to the successful launch of Gmail, which forever changed the email landscape.

This example illustrates how embracing conflict can produce transformative results. Conflict propelled the team to seek compromise and collaboration, laying the groundwork for innovative thinking. When leaders encourage open dialogue and view dissent as an opportunity rather than a threat, they create an environment where ideas can flourish.

To harness conflict effectively, leaders must first cultivate a culture of psychological safety—a term popularized by Harvard Business School professor Amy Edmondson. Psychological safety exists when team members feel safe to take risks and express their opinions without fear of judgment or reprisal. In such an environment, dissent is not only tolerated but celebrated. Employees are empowered to engage in challenging conversations, contributing diverse viewpoints without holding back, knowing that their voices matter.

Consider the renowned software company Atlassian. Known for its collaborative tools like Jira and Confluence, Atlassian's leadership recognized the importance of open dialogue in driving innovation. They implemented regular "Retrospective" meetings, where teams openly discuss what worked, what didn't, and how they can improve going forward. These meetings often spur robust debates, yet they are framed in a way that encourages respect and constructive criticism.

One notable example involved a product team that was working on a new feature. During a retrospective, team members expressed dissatisfaction with the feature's design, arguing that it did not adequately meet user needs. Instead of recoiling from the critiques, team leaders welcomed the feedback, urging their team to dissect the flaws and identify root causes. This conflict led to a complete overhaul of the design, culminating in a much more user-friendly, effective product feature upon release.

Such incidents underscore the premise that when conflict is approached with courage and intention, it can lead to deeper insights and better decision-making. Rather than stifling creativity, dissent can unlock it, propelling teams toward more comprehensive solutions. As seen in both Google and Atlassian's cases, the process of confronting conflict head-on allowed them to leverage diverse perspectives, demonstrating that innovation thrives when diverse voices are not just heard but actively encouraged.

However, leaders must tread carefully; not all conflict is constructive. The key lies in distinguishing between healthy and unhealthy conflict. Healthy conflict is characterized by open-minded engagement, respect for differing viewpoints, and a focus on problem-solving. In contrast, unhealthy conflict manifests as personal attacks, defensiveness, or an unwillingness to listen to others. Leaders must be vigilant in guiding teams toward healthy conflict by promoting active listening, encouraging emotional intelligence, and fostering an atmosphere of mutual respect.

One of the most effective ways to ensure conflicts remain healthy is to establish clear ground rules for discussions. For instance, companies like Pixar utilize a set of communication protocols—structured discussions around ideation and critique are ingrained in their culture. During creative sessions, team members are encouraged to share ideas with the understanding that all feedback is aimed at improving the project, not the individual. By normalizing constructive feedback in this manner, Pixar has produced some of the most beloved animated films in history, even in the face of creative conflicts.

Realigning the focus away from individuals and toward the common goal creates a shared sense of purpose that transcends personal stakes—and this alignment is crucial in maintaining productivity during conflict. It requires leaders to be mindful of group dynamics and facilitate conversations that direct participants toward collaboration, innovation, and growth while carefully sidestepping the pitfalls of belligerent or personal conflicts.

Leaders must also recognize that embracing conflict requires emotional courage. The willingness to engage in potentially uncomfortable conversations reflects a profound commitment to team growth. A personal example can shed light on the impact of this courage.

As a team lead in a previous role within an organization undergoing significant restructuring, I found myself facing mounting conflict distortions within my team. Employees felt uncertain and anxious as departmental changes were implemented, leading to dissent regarding decisions made at the leadership level. Rather than avoiding these conflicts, I called an all-hands meeting, acknowledging the challenge and inviting open dialogue. As tensions rose, I maintained focus on fostering a safe space—encouraging candid discussions around concerns and frustrations. Emotions ran high during parts of the conversation, but the honesty and rawness ultimately uncovered deeper issues that had been festering beneath the surface.

Rather than adopting a defensive stance, I actively listened, empathizing with the struggles my team faced. In establishing a culture where feedback was valued, employees began to share not only their frustrations but also innovative ideas for improvement. We collectively brainstormed and mapped out solutions, leading to changes in our operational processes that benefited the team as a whole. In navigating these conflicts with courage, we found common ground that led to stronger collaboration and mutual understanding—ultimately transforming not just our working dynamics but also boosting morale amongst the team.

This personal experience illustrates how courage in the face of conflict can yield tremendously positive outcomes. It reaffirms that when leaders embrace the potential of constructive conflict, not only can relationships become stronger, but teams can develop innovative solutions that otherwise would have remained hidden.

Handling conflict constructively also fosters a culture of accountability. When team members engage in discussions around challenging topics, they become more cognizant of their contributions to the group dynamic—both positive and negative. This accountability ultimately leads to a more engaged workforce, one that takes ownership of its decisions and outcomes. On the flip side, avoiding difficult conversations cultivates a culture of complacency, coordination failures, and disengagement, which can stymie progress in the long run. By cultivating an environment where team members hold one another accountable through constructive conflict, leaders can instill a culture of continuous improvement.

Let's take a look at a case study from a healthcare organization that exemplifies this process. Faced with a rising number of administrative errors affecting patient care, a team of nurses and administrators gathered to dissect the root causes of the inefficiencies. The meetings began with tension as blame was freely exchanged, showcasing signs of unhealthy conflict. However, over time, as leadership intervened to reframe the discussion toward collaboration, the mood shifted. Team members began to share experiences and acknowledge personal accountability, leading to a fruitful conversation that ultimately identified a series of systemic issues rather than individual failures.

The group embraced constructive conflict as they gathered feedback from different departments and developed collaborative solutions that improved patient care and reduced errors. Establishing regular conflict-resolution workshops became a transformation milestone for the organization. Recognizing the power of constructive conflict, the leadership not only improved team dynamics but also enhanced overall service delivery.

Equipping leaders with the ability to harness conflict as an ally requires training and development. Professional development programs focusing on conflict resolution and effective communication strategies are essential components of cultivating this skill set. Organizations that invest in leadership development not only create more proficient leaders but also foster environments that prioritize transparent communication and teamwork. A study from the Center for Creative Leadership found that organizations with effective leadership development programs are 1.5 times more likely to excel in problem-solving and innovation than their counterparts.

Moreover, it's important to note that fostering collaborative conflict does not imply a constant state of open disagreement—rather, leaders must balance the need for dissent with moments of genuine collaboration. Effective leadership involves knowing when and how to leverage conflict to drive innovation while also creating space for cohesion and trust. Finding this balance may vary within and between organizations, highlighting the crucial role of leadership adaptability.

As a final testament to the power of constructive conflict, consider Southwest Airlines. Historically known for its customer service and employee satisfaction, Southwest embraces a culture of open dissent among flight crews and management. Flight attendants, for example, feel empowered to voice concerns regarding operational safety or customer interactions. Management encourages such dialogue, recognizing that it ultimately leads to a safer, more effective operational environment. This culture has resulted in Southwest maintaining its position as an industry leader despite challenges faced by competitors—showcasing precisely how harnessing conflict can yield measurable success.

In conclusion, the transformational power of constructive conflict cannot be overstated. When leaders possess the courage to embrace dissent, they create pathways to innovation, collaboration, and accountability. The case studies and personal experiences presented herein illustrate that constructive conflict is not merely a necessary evil to be avoided but a powerful ally that, when approached mindfully and courageously, can yield profound benefits for teams and organizations. By fostering a culture that celebrates healthy conflict, leaders enable their teams to thrive, adapting to ever-evolving challenges while ultimately driving sustainable success.

Creating a Culture of Openness

Creating a culture of openness within an organization is fundamental for harnessing conflict as an ally. In an environment where every voice counts, ideas can flourish, creativity can soar, and innovation becomes not just a goal, but a natural outcome of collaborative effort. This subchapter aims to present frameworks that guide leaders and teams in cultivating such environments, drawing from both empirical research and real-world examples.

The Importance of Openness

Openness is more than just a buzzword; it is a powerful catalyst for change in organizational dynamics. When employees feel free to express their thoughts, concerns, and ideas without fear of retribution or dismissal, it fosters a sense of belonging. This belonging significantly enhances team morale and nurtures camaraderie, leading to elevated performance across various metrics. A culture of openness not only encourages engagement but also effectively transforms conflict—a typically disruptive force—into a source of insight and creativity.

To understand the implications of openness, consider a scenario in which team members are hesitant to provide feedback on a project due to concerns about potential backlash. In such situations, leaders might miss critical insights that could inform improvements. However, when openness is embedded in the organizational culture, those same team members would feel empowered to voice their opinions and suggestions, leading to collaborative problem-solving.

Building Frameworks for Openness

Creating a culture of openness requires intentionality and thoughtful frameworks that promote inclusivity. These frameworks can guide organizations in establishing norms and practices that enable meaningful dialogue and diverse perspectives. Here are some effective strategies:

1. Develop Integrative Team Strategies

Integrating teams means fostering relationships where individuals see beyond their roles and connect on a human level. This approach can cultivate an atmosphere of trust and respect, essential for openness. Here are integral components of developing such strategies:

- **Cross-Department Collaboration:** Create opportunities for employees from different departments to work together on projects. This diversity of experience can lead to new perspectives and innovative solutions. Regular interdisciplinary meetings can facilitate rapport-building, which is key to enhancing openness.

- **Diverse Team Building Activities:** Engage in team-building exercises that prioritize communication and collaboration. Activities that require input from all members can break down barriers and encourage individuals to contribute their insights freely.

- **Roles in Dialogue:** Designate roles in team discussions that specifically focus on drawing out quieter voices. Facilitators or champions of inclusion can ensure that everyone has an opportunity to speak, which normalizes contribution from all members, leading to richer discussions.

2. Establish Ongoing Feedback Loops

Feedback is vital for any organization striving towards openness. It must be frequent, constructive, and a two-way street:

- **Regular Check-Ins:** Implement structured check-ins where team members can share their thoughts regarding ongoing projects, team dynamics, or organizational changes. These check-ins can be done weekly or bi-weekly and should provide an avenue for open discussion.

- **Anonymous Feedback Channels:** Create systems that allow employees to provide feedback anonymously if necessary. This can be executed through online surveys or suggestion boxes. Anonymity can be particularly useful for gathering candid insights on sensitive topics.

- **Feedback Culture:** Train employees on how to give and receive feedback constructively. Workshops or training sessions can instill a mindset where feedback is viewed as a growth tool rather than criticism, making it easier for individuals to express themselves openly.

3. Ensure Safe Spaces for Dialogue

Safe spaces are crucial for facilitating open dialogue. Employees should feel secure enough to express dissent without fear of negative consequences. Here's how to cultivate such safe spaces:

- **Encourage Active Listening:** Train leaders to practice active listening, emphasizing that understanding different perspectives is fundamental in communicating openness. The leader's response should reflect genuine engagement with the ideas shared by employees.

Acknowledging their contributions unequivocally reinforces a culture of openness.

- **Conflict Resolution Mechanisms:** Develop clear policies for conflict resolution that uphold respect and fairness when disagreements arise. Employees must know that their concerns will be addressed promptly and appropriately, making them more likely to voice their thoughts.

- **Physical Space Considerations:** Design physical office spaces that encourage casual conversations. Spaces like breakout areas can serve as informal gathering spots, promoting spontaneous discussions that nurture openness.

Real-World Examples

Several organizations exemplify the successful integration of these frameworks:

- **Google:** Known for its innovative culture, Google promotes openness through a variety of channels. Their famous "20% Time" policy encourages employees to spend a portion of their time on passion projects which, combined with cross-department collaboration, cultivates creativity and innovation.

- **Zappos:** This online shoe and clothing retailer thrives on a unique culture of openness, where employees are encouraged to express their ideas even if they go against the grain. By empowering employees through initiatives like open-door policies and transparency in decision-making, Zappos has created an organization that values and utilizes diverse perspectives for growth.

Nurturing Creativity and Growth

Cultivating a culture of openness leads to tangible benefits that extend beyond the surface level. Organizations that prioritize openness tend to see an increase in innovation, productivity, and employee satisfaction:

- **Enhanced Creativity:** When team members feel accepted and valued, they are more likely to share original ideas and solutions. This leads to creative breakthroughs and an organization that is responsive to the changing market landscape.

- **Stronger Problem Solving:** As conflict transforms into constructive dialogue, organizations benefit from diverse viewpoints that contribute to more nuanced problem-solving approaches. A culture of openness nurtures a mindset that views challenges from multiple angles, encouraging innovative solutions to emerge.

- **Increased Employee Engagement:** Employees who feel their voices are heard tend to be more engaged and committed to their organization's mission. They are likely to perform consistently, paving the way for long-term organizational success.

Conclusion

Creating a culture of openness is not a one-time initiative but a continuous commitment to change and improvement. By developing frameworks for team integration, establishing ongoing feedback loops, and ensuring safe spaces for dialogue, leaders can foster an environment where openness thrives. As organizations navigate complexities in the modern business landscape, embracing openness will not only harness conflict as an ally but drive lasting growth and transformation. Through intentional actions and focused strategies, leaders can cultivate a workforce that harnesses the diverse voices and ideas present, positioning their organizations for a future filled with possibility.

Celebrating Conflict Resolution

In the realm of leadership, conflict is often viewed as a challenge—a disruption that must be quashed for the sake of harmony. However, this perspective is fundamentally flawed. Conflict is a natural and necessary part of any organization, an opportunity for growth, innovation, and stronger relationships. As we delve into the narratives that illustrate successful conflict resolution, we will uncover examples of leaders who transformed discord into collaboration, setting a powerful precedent for resilience and teamwork.

An exemplary case of conflict resolution comes from the world of technology, where innovation is both a driving force and a potential source of contention. Consider the story of a renowned CEO of a burgeoning tech startup, Lisa Chen. In her early career, Chen faced a crossroads during a pivotal product development meeting. The team was divided over incorporating two competing technologies into their next software iteration. Half believed the new approach would provide a game-changing functionality, while the other half argued that it would overcomplicate the product and alienate existing users.

Instead of choosing a side, Lisa organized a series of workshops designed to foster open dialogue. She encouraged her team members to voice their concerns without fear of retribution. During one of these sessions, she introduced an unexpected format: a role-reversal exercise, where team members had to argue from the opposing viewpoint. This method not only illuminated underlying assumptions but deepened empathy among team members, as they grappled with the merits and drawbacks of each perspective.

By the end of the workshops, the team achieved a consensus not through suppression of dissent but through rigorous engagement with it. The resolution led to a hybrid solution that integrated both technologies, resulting in a product that exceeded all expectations. The collaborative spirit that emerged from this conflict became a foundation for the company culture, emphasizing that differing opinions could catalyze extraordinary solutions.

Lisa's story serves as a reminder that conflict can spark creativity and innovation. Embracing differing viewpoints, rather than quelling them, fosters an environment where team members feel valued and heard. This approach not only guides organizations to better outcomes but also strengthens the fabric of collaboration, laying the groundwork for future problem-solving endeavors.

The next narrative takes us into the realm of healthcare, where the stakes are often at their highest. In a top-tier hospital, Dr. Sarah Patel, the head of cardiology, faced escalating tension between her department and the surgical team over how to approach a complex patient case. While the cardiologists emphasized a conservative treatment plan based on extensive research, the surgical team advocated for an immediate invasive procedure. The conflicting perspectives led to a standoff that risked not only the patient's well-being but also intra-departmental relationships.

Recognizing the potential fallout, Dr. Patel called for a joint meeting to openly discuss the conflicting opinions, bringing together the key stakeholders from both teams. She framed the conversation around shared goals: the best possible outcome for the patient. Dr. Patel encouraged each party to present their case, complete with data and personal anecdotes relating to past outcomes. This format allowed for a comprehensive evaluation of the issues at hand.

As the discussion unfolded, illuminating moments of agreement emerged. Both teams prioritized patient safety and shared a commitment to excellence. Through the process of sharing and listening, they identified a path forward that integrated both conservative measures and preparedness for surgery if necessary. What had started as a heated conflict transformed into a collaborative care plan that ultimately led to the patient's recovery and strengthened interdepartmental relationships.

Dr. Patel's intervention demonstrated that resolving conflict doesn't necessarily mean finding a compromise where both parties settle for less. Instead, it can involve creating a solution that harnesses the strengths of both perspectives, ensuring that the best possible outcomes are achieved. This experience reinforced the importance of fostering a culture where cross-disciplinary collaboration is celebrated, laying a precedent for how future dilemmas would be approached.

In the world of education, a similar narrative unfolds. High School Principal Anna Garcia encountered resistance when attempting to implement a new curriculum that aimed to foster diversity and inclusion in her school. A vocal group of parents expressed concern that incorporating themes around social justice and equity would distract from the core academic subjects. Rather than avoiding the discomfort, Anna saw an opportunity for engagement.

She organized a town hall meeting where she invited parents, teachers, and students to discuss their concerns openly. The event became a platform for dialogue, where differing perspectives could be articulated and understood. Anna facilitated the conversation, ensuring that each attendee had an opportunity to express their views. As stories was shared—parents recalling experiences of discrimination, teachers discussing the importance of inclusive education, and students describing the value of representation—the room slowly transformed from skepticism to understanding.

In listening to the concerns and fears of her community while also articulating the educational benefits of the new curriculum, Anna was able to build a bridge between divided factions. Over time, the parents recognized the potential for nurturing critical thinkers and compassionate citizens through thoughtful curriculum changes. This town hall approach not only defused tension but also galvanized the community around a shared vision, illustrating how constructive conflict can yield profound understanding and collective progress.

Beyond specific instances of conflict resolution, what the stories of Lisa, Sarah, and Anna have in common is a commitment to celebrating dissent as a precursor to growth. By transforming conflicts into conversations, these leaders fostered environments of trust, where team members felt empowered to voice concerns without fear. Building such a culture is not merely beneficial; it is a strategic imperative in an ever-evolving landscape where collaboration and creativity are essential.

As we look toward the broader implications of these narratives, the significance of celebrating conflict resolution within organizations becomes clear. The cultivation of an open dialogue fosters not just a more inclusive atmosphere but also enhances resilience. Organizations that prioritize conflict resolution as a pathway to teamwork and innovation are better positioned to navigate challenges, adapt to change, and involve all voices in shaping their future.

To further illustrate this point, we must explore how various organizations have institutionalized the principles of conflict resolution into their daily operations. One such example comes from the financial sector, where the CEO of a leading investment firm, Tom Richards, implemented a Conflict Resolution Coach program. This initiative trained employees across all levels in essential skills for resolving disputes and having difficult conversations.

Through workshops that included role-playing exercises, case studies, and conflict resolution strategies, team members learned how to approach conflicts proactively. Rather than viewing disagreements as negatives, employees began to see them as learning experiences—elements crucial to growth and development. The program led not only to a reduction in interpersonal conflicts but also improved team performance, as colleagues communicated more effectively, shared ideas openly, and collaborated seamlessly.

The success of the Conflict Resolution Coach program underlines the potency of proactive conflict management. It encourages individuals to take responsibility for their contributions to conflicts, fostering a culture of accountability and openness. Moreover, the training provides a tangible framework within which employees can navigate challenging relationships, ultimately setting a standard for mutual respect and collaboration in our workplaces.

This continuous investment in conflict resolution cultivates a learning organization where challenges are accepted as opportunities rather than threats. Teams become adept at navigating the tumultuous waters of disagreement, emerging stronger and more united on the other side. They are equipped with the skills necessary to facilitate dialogues that honor individual experiences while focusing on collective goals.

In considering how conflict resolution can be celebrated effectively, it is essential to create mechanisms that recognize and reward constructive engagement. Organizations can host "Conflict Resolution Celebrations," where teams can share their conflict resolution stories, recognize the effort put forth, and celebrate the diversity of perspectives that ultimately contributed to success. By publicly acknowledging instances of conflict resolution, organizations send a strong message about the value of dissent and the importance of maintaining strong partnerships.

When employees know that their voices are valued and their dissent is respected, they are more likely to engage authentically and contribute whole-heartedly to problem-solving efforts. This recognition creates a self-reinforcing cycle of open dialogue—where fear dissipates, engagement flourishes, and innovation thrives.

The climate of collaboration fostered through celebrating conflict resolution also extends to encouraging risk-taking. In agile organizations, where adaptability is crucial, leaders must inspire teams to embrace calculated risks. When teams are equipped to handle internal dissent with confidence, they become more likely to propose unorthodox ideas and challenge established norms, knowing that dissent will be met with respect and constructive discourse.

Head of Innovation at a multinational corporation, Kendra Lee, embodied this principle when she encouraged her team to experiment with different approaches to product design. Understanding that creativity often arises from friction, she promoted a culture where team members could vocalize opposing opinions and engage in lively discussions. As a result, her team developed pioneering products that not only stood out in the market but also reflected the diverse perspectives of the individuals involved in the design process.

Kendra's leadership style celebrates the richness of conflict resolution, ultimately driving innovation and cementing her team's place as industry frontrunners. Her approach illustrates that by inviting dissent and creating spaces for disagreement, organizations can unleash a world of creativity and possibility.

As we synthesize these collected narratives, we arrive at a powerful conclusion: conflict, when embraced as an ally, gives rise to remarkable opportunities for teamwork and resilience. Leaders who celebrate conflict resolution not only elevate the dynamics within their organizations but also inspire others to approach challenging discussions with openness and courage.

Moving forward, it is incumbent upon current and aspiring leaders to foster environments where conflict is not merely tolerated but celebrated. By actively engaging dissent and recognizing the strength that lies within differing opinions, organizations can create cultures that prioritize collaboration, engagement, and innovation.

In doing so, they empower themselves to navigate the complexities of leadership in today's fast-paced world. Leaders should consider the stories shared here as not just isolated successes but rather as guiding principles for their leadership journeys. The invitation is clear: embrace conflict, celebrate resolution, and watch as teams flourish and organizations thrive.

CHAPTER SIX

THE PATH TO SUSTAINABLE CHANGE

Embracing Change as a Constant

In today's fast-paced and ever-evolving landscape, the notion of change is not merely an event that organizations endure; it has become a constant that shapes every aspect of existence in the business world. Organizations that successfully navigate change emerge stronger, more adaptive, and increasingly competitive. The stories of leaders who have embraced change reveal a wealth of lessons about resilience, agility, and the continuous cycle of learning that should be inherent in any successful organization.

Consider the case of a global technology firm that faced a seismic shift in its competitive landscape with the rapid rise of artificial intelligence. Long known for its traditional software solutions, the company found itself grappling with the need to pivot towards AI-driven products. Initial resistance from employees was palpable; many were entrenched in a mindset that valued stability over innovation. However, the leadership team recognized change, driven by market demands, was inevitable. They understood that inaction was not an option.

To facilitate this transition, the leadership chose to communicate openly with their teams, creating a culture of transparency about the challenges ahead. The leadership team organized workshops where employees were encouraged to voice their concerns, share their ideas, and collaborate on new projects aimed at integrating AI technologies into existing products. This collaborative approach not only eased the anxiety surrounding change but fostered a sense of ownership among employees, making them more invested in the outcomes of their transformations.

Through iterative testing of new products and soliciting continuous feedback from users, this organization began to see growth trajectories that surpassed earlier expectations. Within just two years, the company reported not only improved product lines but also a refreshed corporate culture where agility became a foundational value. What began as a daunting challenge had morphed into an opportunity for empowering employees and transforming company identity, thus illustrating the crucial lesson: adapting to change drives not just survival but also unprecedented growth.

Another compelling narrative occurs in the manufacturing sector, where a mid-sized firm struggled against increasing international competition and rising costs. Instead of resigning themselves to a shrinking market share, the leadership team chose to embrace a lean manufacturing philosophy. This transition began with intensive training sessions, where employees at every level learned how to identify wasteful processes and improve efficiency.

Initially, resistance emerged. Long-held traditions and methods might have appeared more comfortable than the unknown pathways of lean principles. However, through the dialogue fostered by the leadership, employees started to understand the long-term benefits. Leaders illustrated how lean manufacturing could ultimately lead to job security rather than layoffs. As the culture shifted, employees became advocates for change rather than bystanders.

As the months passed, the results were transformational. The company became more responsive to customer demands and had significantly reduced production times. This adaptation not only enhanced the organization's competitiveness but also cultivated employee morale—a critical factor for securing their dedication and creativity. The manufacturing firm's experience highlights another vital insight: change is not merely an operational necessity but a vital opportunity for engagement, fostering a culture that thrives on innovation and continuous improvement.

In the world of healthcare, another case exemplifies the necessity of embracing change. A prominent hospital system faced unprecedented challenges during a global pandemic. The traditional patient care models were upended as the healthcare landscape shifted drastically overnight, requiring flexibility and innovation. The leadership recognized the urgent need for their staff to transition towards telehealth services, a shift that many had previously viewed as impractical.

To ensure a successful transition, leaders initiated comprehensive training sessions tailored to equip clinicians with the necessary digital skills. Regular meetings helped to uncover potential barriers, allowing staff to voice concerns and contribute ideas for improvement. The result was astonishing. Not only was the hospital system able to maintain care levels during peak surges, but they were also able to expand their reach to patients who had difficulty accessing in-person services prior to the change.

This adaptive approach allowed the hospital to emerge from the crisis not only intact but also with a newly adopted model that would streamline processes long after the immediate crisis had passed. Reflecting on their journey, healthcare leaders articulated invaluable insights about the power of adaptability, reiterating that embracing change helped their teams not just survive a crisis but also innovate new methods of care delivery that would continue to benefit their communities.

Not all journeys through change, however, progress smoothly and without challenge. In fact, observing the complexities surrounding an organization's adaptation reveals a tapestry woven with lessons that focus not just on success but also on how failures can serve as powerful catalysts for future growth. Consider a retail chain that underwent a comprehensive rebranding effort to capture a younger demographic. While the ambition was admirable and generated excitement initially, the execution faltered, with employees unsure of how to implement the new changes and customers resistant to altering their perceptions.

The leadership team quickly recognized the disconnect and prioritized gathering feedback from both employees and customers in a series of open forums. These candid conversations opened a critical dialogue; employees expressed their confusion about the new brand identity, while customers shared their pre-existing loyalty to the old brand. Armed with this valuable feedback, the leaders re-evaluated their strategy, pivoted their marketing angle, and refocused efforts on fostering community connections. They invited loyal customers back into the fold, emphasizing their legacy while seamlessly introducing the new brand elements.

Slowly, as employees were equipped with the insights needed to communicate the rebranding effectively, they found renewed energy in their roles, ultimately leading to a successful relaunch. The case highlights an essential truth: change is as much about communication and empathy as it is about the structural adjustments being made. The retail ensemble demonstrated that committing to a dialogic approach helped not only in overcoming initial setbacks but also led to deeper relationships forged between leadership and employees—a vital component for fostering a thriving organization.

A further aspect of embracing change lies in recognizing that every transition presents an opportunity for growth. Consider a non-profit organization aiming to enhance its financial sustainability. The leadership identified a prevailing culture that relied heavily on government funding—a configuration proving increasingly vulnerable amid shifting political landscapes.

Instead of resigning to an uncertain future, the organization embarked on a multifaceted transformation by diversifying revenue streams. Leadership encouraged employees to brainstorm innovative fundraising initiatives, resulting in striking campaigns that engaged broader communities. The collaborative brainstorming process yielded results beyond financial benefit, reigniting passion among employees and reinforcing their shared purpose.

With a dynamic shift toward community-oriented initiatives, this transformation not only stabilized revenue but also reinvigorated employee engagement and connection to mission-oriented work. Leaders emerged not merely as figureheads but rather as facilitators of shared vision, demonstrating to their teams that embracing change creates extensively positive ripple effects.

As these case studies illustrate, at the essence of every change lies the invitation to learn. Leaders who foster an environment where questioning is encouraged and where mistakes are viewed as learning opportunities cultivate a culture that thrives. Learning through change necessitates that leaders actively promote resilience, articulating strong support systems for their teams to ensure that each change initiative is explored with a mindset open to growth.

Moreover, investing in continuous learning opportunities allows organizations to navigate the turbulent waters of change more effectively. Regular training sessions, mentorship programs, and knowledge-sharing platforms can empower employees to adapt and enhance their skills, ensuring their readiness for both expected and unexpected changes. Organizations benefit by integrating a learning-based approach that champions curiosity and innovation, thus enhancing the internal capacity to embrace change.

It is also essential for leaders to model adaptive behavior themselves. A leadership posture that embraces vulnerability and acknowledges imperfections creates a sense of trust and belonging within teams. Leaders who openly discuss their experiences navigating change, their own learning curves, and the occasional missteps can inspire employees to possess similar courage. Vulnerability becomes a facilitator of authenticity, encouraging employees to voice their concerns while remaining open to innovative ideas.

As leaders guide their teams through cycles of change, weaving a narrative that emphasizes growth amid challenges is crucial. Celebrating small wins and recognizing individual contributions creates momentum that propels the change process further. By positioning change as an ongoing journey rather than a destination, leaders set the tone for adaptability, emphasizing that evolution is a continual process that thrives on exploration and curiosity.

Ultimately, organizations that choose to embrace change as a constant reap rewards that far surpass the challenges they encounter. As they transition through various phases, lessons learned during each shift furnish insights that refine strategy and drive growth. Continuous learning emerges not merely as a byproduct but as a business imperative—ensuring teams are adept at tackling new landscapes and capitalizing on emerging opportunities.

In closing, leaders navigating the complexities of change must cultivate a resilience-oriented mindset, allowing for adaptation and fostering a culture that prioritizes learning. The stories shared throughout this narrative underscore that organizations are not defined solely by their successes but by their ability to pivot and learn from adversity. As the business environment continues to shift at unprecedented speeds, those who embrace change as a constant will find themselves well-equipped to thrive in the face of uncertainty, fostering sustainable practices that support long-term growth and innovation.

Resilient Leadership Cultures

In the fast-paced world of modern business, adaptability and resilience have emerged as the cornerstones of successful leadership cultures. Leaders today find themselves navigating an unpredictable landscape where change is not just likely, but inevitable. The ability to pivot swiftly in response to market shifts, evolving technologies, and dynamic workforce needs is paramount. Organizations that embed these qualities into their core values and practices cultivate an environment where both leaders and employees can thrive.

A resilient leadership culture is characterized by a commitment to continuous improvement and a proactive approach to change. This shift from a static mindset to one that embraces agility enables organizations to respond to challenges not with fear but with optimism and a forward-thinking perspective. Resilient leaders, instilling this culture, recognize that true strength lies not in avoiding failure but in learning from it. They encourage experimentation, accept mistakes as part of the growth process, and celebrate innovation.

One organization that exemplifies this notion is Zappos, known for its customer service excellence and strong organizational culture. Zappos emphasizes the importance of employee empowerment—a key ingredient in fostering resilience. By allowing employees the autonomy to make decisions and take risks, Zappos fosters an environment where individuals feel secure in expressing themselves and testing new ideas. Their commitment to a core set of values, including 'Create Fun and A Little Weirdness' and 'Be Adventurous, Creative, and Open-Minded,' demonstrates a cultural foundation that encourages creativity and adaptability. Employees know that their ideas will be valued, even if they don't always succeed.

Generous support for learning and development is another hallmark of resilient organizations. Through ongoing training, mentorship programs, and leadership development initiatives, these organizations equip their workforce with the skills necessary to respond to future challenges. For example, a study on the tech giant Google highlights their investment in continuous learning as a strategic advantage. Google has cultivated a growth mindset across the board, with initiatives that encourage employees to learn from one another and take ownership of their skill development. Such practices not only enhance individual capabilities but also promote a collaborative culture where knowledge-sharing becomes the norm.

Moreover, resilient leadership recognizes the importance of cultivating psychological safety within teams. Amy Edmondson, a Harvard Business School professor and leading researcher on psychological safety, explains that fostering an environment where team members feel safe to take risks, express ideas, and voice concerns is essential for innovation. In a psychologically safe environment, employees are more likely to share their thoughts without fear of reprimand or judgment. Well-known companies like Pixar have successfully created such cultures. At Pixar, a culture of open communication is encouraged, with regular feedback loops and brainstorming sessions where no idea is too outlandish to explore. This openness not only enhances creativity but also builds resilience by allowing the company to navigate challenges collaboratively.

In addition to individual and team-focused approaches, resilient cultures prioritize transparency and inclusivity. Leaders are open about organizational challenges, fostering trust and allowing employees to feel more invested in the collective journey. Transparency encourages employees to share their insights and solutions, fostering a two-way dialogue where employees feel genuinely involved in the organization's direction. Patagonia, the outdoor clothing company, embodies this principle through its commitment to social responsibility and environmental sustainability. By sharing their challenges and progress toward sustainability goals openly, they engage employees in their mission, fostering a united front that inspires resilience and adaptability among all members.

Effective leaders also understand the need for change management strategies that prioritize resilience. Change can be disruptive, and leaders must guide their teams with empathy and clarity during transitions. Satya Nadella, CEO of Microsoft, recognized this when he took the helm of the tech giant. Under his leadership, Microsoft underwent a cultural transformation centered around collaboration, innovation, and employee growth. Through initiatives such as the 'Growth Mindset' philosophy, Nadella empowered employees to embrace challenges and learning opportunities, constantly pushing the organization toward new heights. Microsoft established a culture where adaptability became ingrained in every level—from senior leadership to entry-level positions.

Beyond personal growth, leaders must also foster resilience within the systems and processes of the organization. This involves designing workflows that allow for flexibility and adaptability. Take the example of Agile methodologies applied in software development: Agile prioritizes iterative cycles, allowing teams to adapt to changing requirements quickly. This framework not only enhances productivity but also prepares leaders and teams to embrace change, continuously refining their approaches based on feedback and emerging trends. The evolving business environment requires a shift in mindsets—from rigid structures to frameworks that embrace change, ensuring teams are equipped to respond effectively.

Feedback mechanisms, too, are vital in nurturing a resilient leadership culture. Organizations that prioritize open channels for feedback demonstrate commitment to improvement and adaptability. These mechanisms can include employee surveys, performance reviews, or even anonymous suggestions that empower individuals to voice opinions. An example of effective feedback practice can be observed at Adobe, where the annual performance review process has been replaced by ongoing 'Check-In' meetings between managers and employees. This shift emphasizes frequent dialogue and feedback, actively engaging employees in their development while fostering an atmosphere of continuous improvement.

Furthermore, celebrating successes—big and small—plays a significant role in reinforcing a resilient leadership culture. Acknowledging achievements cultivates a shared sense of purpose, motivating teams to stay engaged and focused amid challenges. Salesforce, a key player in customer relationship management, promotes recognition through various employee engagement programs, including a monthly 'Ohana' award that celebrates individuals embodying the company's core values. By doing so, Salesforce fosters a culture of appreciation, resilience, and commitment to ongoing progress.

As the landscape of leadership continues to evolve, organizations must remain vigilant about fostering a culture of resilience and adaptability. Continuous learning, transparent communication, psychological safety, and celebrating successes—all play into cultivating resilient leadership. The onus lies on leaders not only to champion these values themselves but to ensure that every individual within the organization feels empowered to partake in the culture.

But in the pursuit of a resilient culture, challenges will inevitably arise. Leaders must recognize that the journey is not linear; adaptation takes time and requires a commitment to long-term change. Organizations that fail to embrace the inherent challenges associated with establishing a resilient culture may find themselves stagnating, watching as competitors take the lead.

In conclusion, the path to building resilient leadership cultures is shaped by deliberate efforts to embrace adaptability, prioritize psychological safety, and foster open communication. Today's successful leaders must not only navigate challenges but also instill a sense of collective responsibility among their teams—encouraging everyone to share in the journey of transformation and growth. By embedding these values into their organizational DNA, they will equip themselves and their teams with the resilience to not only withstand change but to thrive in the face of it.

Measuring Impact

In today's rapidly changing business landscape, the ability to measure impact effectively has become a key component of sustainable leadership. Metrics serve as the navigational compass for organizations seeking long-term success; they provide the insight needed to assess whether changes are yielding the desired outcomes and how these changes resonate within the organizational ecosystem. Understanding how to effectively measure impact requires a blend of quantitative and qualitative assessments, as both are essential to achieving a holistic view of organizational health.

To grasp how these metrics come into play, we begin by exploring several key categories that can guide evaluation efforts: performance indicators, employee engagement metrics, customer satisfaction scores, and adaptability measures. Each of these categories plays a vital role in determining how well an organization responds to implemented changes and adapts to its environment.

Performance Indicators

Performance indicators serve as the backbone for measuring impact. Key Performance Indicators (KPIs) allow organizations to ascertain whether they are on track in relation to their strategic goals. The criteria for selecting effective KPIs can differ greatly depending on the industry and specific organizational objectives; however, certain foundational elements remain constant. For instance, KPIs should be Specific, Measurable, Achievable, Relevant, and Time-bound (SMART).

A well-structured KPI framework could include metrics like revenue growth rate, profit margin, and market share. The interplay of these numbers can reveal patterns over time, allowing leaders to determine whether specific changes, such as a new marketing strategy or product line, have positively impacted the organization's standing in the market.

Case Study: A tech startup focused on enhancing its market positioning decided to shift its customer engagement strategy by incorporating a data-driven approach. By implementing a new KPI framework, the organization was able to track customer acquisition costs, customer lifetime value, and churn rates. Analyzing these KPIs unveiled that their investment in customer feedback loops was driving significant improvement in customer retention and satisfaction, ultimately leading to a 30% increase in profitability within a year.

This example underscores the importance of not only selecting the right KPIs but also maintaining a continuous evaluation process based on feedback. Organizations must fine-tune these metrics as necessary, evolving them alongside changing market conditions and business objectives.

Employee Engagement Metrics

In tandem with performance indicators, evaluating employee engagement is a crucial aspect of measuring impact, particularly when navigating organizational change. Engaged employees are motivated, productive, and aligned with the company's vision. Metrics like employee Net Promoter Score (eNPS), turnover rates, and engagement survey results paint a clearer picture of the organizational climate.

A strategic focus on employee engagement can yield substantial dividends. Organizations that prioritize feedback and act on employees' insights tend to exhibit higher retention rates and productivity levels. Regular check-ins can present opportunities for employees to express their opinions, thereby enhancing organizational communication.

Case Study: An HR manager at a mid-sized manufacturing firm chose to implement quarterly engagement surveys aimed at understanding employee sentiment regarding a recent shift in company policy. The surveys highlighted concerns about workload and resources, as well as opportunities for team collaboration. Once the organization acted on the feedback by redistributing project responsibilities and setting aside time for team brainstorming sessions, employee morale visibly improved, leading to a 15% rise in overall productivity over six months.

Customer Satisfaction Scores

Organizations also need to prioritize customer satisfaction metrics as they measure the impact of changes on the external perception of a company. Metrics such as Net Promoter Score (NPS), Customer

Satisfaction Score (CSAT), and Customer Effort Score (CES) gauge how well customers feel their needs are being met.

Often drawing on insights from customer feedback, these metrics help leaders understand how changes in the organization resonate with their clientele. They also enable leaders to establish a direct line to customers' sentiments, allowing organizations to identify areas for improvement or innovation.

Case Study: Consider a retail company that recently redesigned its online shopping platform. By deploying customer satisfaction surveys pre- and post-launch, they were able to monitor the impact of the redesign on user experience. While initial feedback showed a surge in satisfaction rates, deeper analysis of NPS indicated a segment of customers was still facing challenges during the checkout process. Using this feedback, the company refined aspects of their website, ultimately improving customer satisfaction ratings by 35% over the subsequent quarter.

Adaptability Measures

Another vital aspect of measuring impact in any organization is assessing adaptability. Organizations are not static entities; they constantly evolve in response to both internal developments and external pressures. Metrics that gauge adaptability include response times to market changes, the number of innovations introduced, and the overall speed of decision-making processes.

Adaptability measures provide leaders with insights into how well their organizations are positioned to navigate change. These may often hinge on leadership practices, as leaders set the tone for agility within their teams. Adaptability can therefore be assessed through both qualitative feedback and quantitative metrics, enabling organizations to track how effectively they can pivot in response to emerging opportunities and challenges.

Case Study: A financial services firm faced a market downturn that led to an urgent need for adaptability. By implementing a robust feedback mechanism that encouraged innovative ideas from all employee levels, the organization was able to introduce new financial products that catered to changing consumer behaviors. The response time to market for their new offerings improved by 40%, demonstrating resilience during adverse conditions. The company saw its market share increase and felt more prepared to handle future market fluctuations.

Combining the Metrics

While the aforementioned metrics can provide meaningful insight individually, the true power of measuring impact lies in synthesizing these data points. A multidimensional approach clarifies the interdependencies amongst performance indicators, employee engagement levels, customer satisfaction, and adaptability. Coupling qualitative insights with quantitative analysis paints a broader and more intricate picture of an organization's performance.

For example, a sudden drop in customer satisfaction scores might correlate with disengaged employees or a lack of adaptability to customer needs, highlighting interrelated challenges. Recognizing these patterns positions leaders to take a holistic view of organizational challenges and empower them to develop comprehensive strategies responsive to the interconnected nature of these metrics.

Strategic Implementation of Insights

Insights gained from these metrics should not merely sit in reports or dashboards; organizations must proactively implement the findings. A successful feedback loop entails translating metrics into actionable strategies that align closely with the organization's broader goals.

Frequent follow-ups on implemented changes delineate how their introduction has enhanced organizational outcomes, or if efforts fell short of expectations. Clear communication keeps all stakeholders aligned, building a culture that centers around continuous improvement.

Further, organizations should encourage a culture of accountability, where leaders respectfully own the insights provided by metrics. By nurturing transparency, they can bolster trust in the organization, fostering a collective sense of responsibility for objectives and outcomes.

Fostering a Feedback Culture

To create a thriving ecosystem for measuring impact, organizations must encourage a culture of feedback at all levels. This climate promotes shared accountability for both successes and shortcomings, creating a sense of ownership throughout the organization. Employees and stakeholders must recognize that their opinions matter, leading to robust discussions, innovative problem-solving, and an environment conducive to growth.

Integrating regular feedback sessions where individuals can voice their opinions around organizational changes nurtures a culture of openness. These sessions facilitate honest dialogue, allowing teams to pivot quickly and make necessary adjustments while boosting morale and productivity.

Personal Responsibility for Metrics

Leaders must also take personal responsibility for their respective metrics, understanding that their performance directly influences organizational outcomes. This accountability should extend downward, with team leaders encouraged to evaluate their subsection's progress.

Leaders who model this behavior create a ripple effect, inspiring others within their teams to embrace shared accountability and invigorate a culture where leaders and team members alike are aligned toward collective success.

Evaluating the Evaluation Process

Finally, organizations should regularly assess the methods employed to measure impact. Change is an ever-present reality; therefore, metrics should evolve along with internal and external conditions. Periodic reviews of existing metrics ensure they remain relevant and continue to serve organizational goals effectively.

Conducting a thorough evaluation of the evaluation process may yield insights into areas of improvement and potential new metrics worth exploring. Encouraging teams to share best practices can forge stronger links across the organization, thereby enhancing overall performance and fostering a cohesive approach towards sustainable change.

Conclusion

Measuring impact is not a one-off endeavor but rather an ongoing process that requires vigilance, adaptability, and commitment. By implementing a structured approach to assess performance indicators, employee engagement, customer satisfaction, and adaptability, organizations can navigate the complex landscape of change with purpose and precision.

Ultimately, when feedback is actively sought and acted upon, organizations become more resilient and agile. With the right metrics as their guide, leaders can create a sustainable path forward, fostering environments of growth and innovation that propel not only the organization but its people toward future successes.

CHAPTER SEVEN

PRIDE IN PROGRESS, NOT PERFECTION

Navigating Achievements

In the ever-evolving landscape of leadership, one fundamental truth emerges: the path to achievement is often riddled with complexity and uncertainty. Leaders are charged not just with reaching destinations but also with cultivating environments that foster growth and progress. The hallmark of effective leadership lies in an acute understanding that every step taken, every milestone reached, is a testament to both individual and collective effort. However, the age-old pursuit of perfection often obscures these critical achievements, leading many to overlook the significance of progress in favor of an unattainable ideal.

To adequately address this phenomenon, we first need to understand the psychological implications of focusing solely on perfection. The relentless pursuit of a perfect standard can stifle innovation, creativity, and, ultimately, the morale of the entire team. When leaders express perfectionism, they inadvertently create a culture where fear of failure reigns, talent goes unrecognized, and potential is never fully realized. In contrast, when leaders prioritize acknowledging progress, they inspire their teams by reinforcing the value of incremental achievements and setting the stage for continuous improvement.

Celebrating Progress

Celebrating progress involves a deliberate recognition of the milestones that create a path toward the ultimate goals leaders aim to achieve. This recognition should be both vocal and visible—individuals and teams need to feel appreciated for their contributions. Celebrating progress fosters a sense of belonging, motivates individuals to strive for improvement, and cultivates a culture where success is measured by personal and collective development rather than merely by end results.

Take the case of a tech start-up that embarked on creating innovative software solutions. As they faced various challenges, the leadership recognized that big leaps toward their ambitious vision could be disheartening when success seemed distant. Instead of only applauding the final product, they implemented regular check-ins to celebrate each minor achievement: a successful debug, an increase in user engagement, or completing a vital phase of development. Such acknowledgment not only bolstered morale but also transformed the team's perception of their work. They began viewing challenges as opportunities—an outlook that infused excitement into their daily tasks.

The role of recognition cannot be overstated. Public acknowledgment of achievements—no matter how small—can energize a team, instilling a sense of accomplishment and accountability. Implementing this practice may include team meetings, bulletin boards, or even digital platforms dedicated to sharing successes. Leaders can create a culture where progress, however minute, is celebrated, thus reinforcing a positive cycle of motivation and achievement.

The Importance of Milestones

Setting and recognizing milestones is a strategic element of celebrating progress. By breaking down large, overarching goals into smaller, manageable objectives, leaders can relieve the pressure of perfectionism and establish a clearer roadmap toward success. Milestones not only serve as markers of progress; they also provide teams with a way to visualize their journey, fostering ongoing motivation.

For example, a company focused on launching a new product might break the process down into distinct phases: research, development, testing, and launch. Celebrating the completion of each phase emphasizes the incremental progress made instead of focusing solely on the successful launch as the sole indicator of achievement. Each completed phase is a victory in itself, encouraging teams to remain engaged and invested in the process.

This strategy applies well in project management settings, where methodologies such as Agile are employed. Agile emphasizes iterative development and regular feedback loops. Teams assess their progress at the end of each sprint—recognized periods of work—allowing them to adapt their strategies and celebrate small victories along the way. This approach does not just prioritize the endpoint; it highlights the importance of continuous movement toward a goal, creating a more resilient and adaptable team.

Embracing Challenges for Future Growth

While celebrating progress is vital, it must be coupled with a mindset that encourages embracing future challenges. Achievements, no matter how significant, should serve as a launchpad for continual growth rather than an endpoint in themselves. Leaders can facilitate this by fostering an environment where learning from experiences, both victorious and challenging, is valued.

Encouraging a growth mindset is crucial for a successful transition from celebrating progress to embracing future challenges. A growth mindset—the belief that abilities and intelligence can be developed—encourages individuals to learn from feedback and view failures as opportunities for growth. This mindset directly correlates with resilience, which is essential in navigating the complex dynamics of leadership and organizational development.

Leaders can create this learning culture by sharing their own developmental journeys, discussing challenges they've faced, and how they learned and evolved from those experiences. This practice not only humanizes leaders but also reinforces the belief that setbacks are not failures—they are significant opportunities to grow. When team members observe their leaders embracing challenges rather than shying away from them, they are more likely to adopt a similar approach.

Team reflections on past projects, both successful and unsuccessful, can serve as another means of reinforcing this growth mindset.

Facilitating dedicated sessions where teams can critically assess their performance allows for open conversations about what worked, what didn't, and how they can improve moving forward. This reflective practice cultivates an atmosphere of learning and growth, encouraging employees to take on challenges with confidence.

Strategies to Cultivate Achievement Focused Leadership

For leaders aiming to champion a culture that prioritizes progress, several strategies can be employed:

1. **Establish Clear Objectives:** Define metrics that highlight both performance outcomes and quality of improvement. Objectives should align with a broader organizational vision, allowing progress to be contextualized within a meaningful framework.

2. **Recognize and Celebrate Incremental Success:** Institute regular celebrations of progress, whether through informal shout-outs, formal recognition programs, or team-building activities. Ensure that recognition is genuine and tailored to individuals' contributions.

3. **Visualize Progress:** Utilize visual tools such as charts or dashboards that depict team and individual milestones. This visual representation provides a tangible understanding of the journey and instills a sense of pride in the collective progress made.

4. **Facilitate Continuous Feedback:** Implement robust feedback mechanisms that encourage employees to share insights on performance and areas for improvement. Encourage leaders to solicit feedback about their leadership styles to foster an environment of openness.

5. **Promote Learning and Development Opportunities:** Foster an environment that encourages skill development and lifelong learning. Offer resources—be it through workshops, mentorship, or online courses—that can help team members build their capabilities in alignment with organizational goals.

6. **Create Safe Spaces for Failure:** Establish trust within the team so that individuals feel safe to take risks and voice their concerns without fear of retribution. Valuing insight from failures can catalyze innovation

and alignment with the overarching goals.

7. **Engaging in Reflective Practices:** Set aside time for team members to reflect on their contributions and experiences. Utilize methods like post-mortem analysis to evaluate completed projects—spotlighting both successes and lessons learned.

Ultimately, the goal of navigating achievements is not merely about checking off accomplishments but embracing a mindset—one that celebrates growth, learning, and perseverance. Leaders play a pivotal role in shaping this mindset within their teams; by aligning recognition with a culture of continuous improvement, they can transform the narrative around achievements.

Leading with a focus on progress cultivates an optimistic environment where innovation and collaboration thrive. It not only affirms individual and collective efforts but also lays a foundation for sustainable success.

In conclusion, the journey of leadership is one where acknowledging milestones, embracing future challenges, and celebrating incremental progress converges. By shifting the focus from perfectionism to appreciation of achievements, leaders can inspire their teams to persevere, explore new horizons, and redefine their limits. This transformative approach ultimately generates a powerful ripple effect—one where the celebration of progress becomes a catalyst for extraordinary achievements.

As leaders navigate their own paths and influence their teams, the art of celebrating progress will remain an enduring necessity in an unpredictable world, serving as both a guiding compass and a source of inspiration. By continuously fostering a culture that cultivates and celebrates achievements, leaders ensure not just survival amidst challenges but, indeed, the thriving future of their organizations.

A Culture of Agility

In today's rapidly changing landscape, the need for agility within leadership roles cannot be overstated. Organizations that cling to rigid structures and processes often find themselves ill-equipped to navigate the complexities of modern business environments. Agility is not merely a buzzword; it is a vital competency that empowers leaders to respond to challenges and opportunities with grace and efficacy. By fostering a culture of agility, leaders not only enhance their own effectiveness but also inspire their teams to embrace change as a source of strength rather than a potential threat.

The significance of being agile and adaptable lies in the very nature of change itself. Change is constant, and a leader's capacity to adapt to evolving circumstances defines their success. This adaptability is not about abandoning principles or compromising values, but about recognizing the fluidity of reality and adjusting strategies accordingly. This section will delve into the cognitive frameworks that support agile leadership as well as share real-world testimonials from contemporary leaders who have successfully embraced change over the rigid pursuit of perfection.

To understand agility in leadership, one must first examine the cognitive frameworks that facilitate adaptability. These frameworks provide a mental blueprint that guides decision-making and action in the face of uncertainty. One such framework is the concept of "growth mindset" introduced by psychologist Carol Dweck. A growth mindset posits that abilities and intelligence can be developed through dedication and hard work. This fundamental belief fosters resilience, openness to feedback, and an eagerness to learn.

Leaders who embody a growth mindset are more likely to embrace challenges and view failures as opportunities for growth rather than setbacks. They encourage their teams to take calculated risks and experiment with novel approaches, engendering an environment where creativity can flourish. For example, during a significant product launch at a technology startup, the leadership team faced unexpected challenges. Rather than dwelling on failed attempts, they gathered feedback, reassessed their strategies, and made iterative improvements. This adaptability not only salvaged the product launch but also led to a successful market entry that surpassed initial expectations.

Another critical cognitive framework that enhances agility in leaders is the principle of "adaptive leadership." This approach, pioneered by Ron Heifetz and Marty Linsky, emphasizes the importance of addressing adaptive challenges instead of merely technical problems. Technical problems are solvable through existing solutions, whereas adaptive challenges require leaders to engage their teams in the process of learning and managing change.

Adaptive leaders recognize that leadership is not about providing all the answers but facilitating a collective exploration of solutions. They empower teams to confront dilemmas head-on and develop innovative approaches to complex issues. This participatory style cultivates a sense of ownership among team members, enhancing their commitment to the organization's goals. Leaders who practiced adaptive leadership during the COVID-19 pandemic illustrated its effectiveness vividly. Many organizations, faced with unprecedented disruptions, had to rethink their operational models completely. Leaders who consulted with their teams on shifting dynamics developed creative solutions that allowed their organizations to pivot quickly, from remote work arrangements to innovative service offerings.

Equally important is the ability to cultivate a psychologically safe environment where team members feel empowered to voice their thoughts, ideas, and concerns without fear of retribution. Psychological safety, as defined by Amy Edmondson, allows individuals to express themselves freely and take risks. In a psychologically safe culture, leaders demonstrate vulnerability and openness, reinforcing the belief that every team member's contribution is valuable and significant.

When a leader promotes psychological safety, they create a platform for honest dialogue where feedback flows seamlessly in both directions. This openness fosters adaptability by enabling teams to share lessons learned from both successes and failures. For instance, a leader at a healthcare organization prioritized psychological safety and regularly held feedback sessions to encourage team members to share their insights. As a result, when the organization faced challenges in delivering patient services during the pandemic, the team was able to quickly brainstorm solutions, leveraging collective knowledge. Their agility in harnessing diverse perspectives led to rapid process improvements, benefiting both patients and staff.

While cognitive frameworks lay the groundwork for agility, real-world testimonials from contemporary leaders offer invaluable insights into the practical applications of these principles. Consider the experience of Angela, a regional manager at a multinational consumer goods company. Faced with a significant market shift driven by changing consumer preferences, Angela knew that remaining stagnant could jeopardize her team's competitive edge.

Drawing upon her growth mindset, Angela instinctively reframed the challenge. Instead of viewing the new consumer trends as a threat to their established products, she positioned them as an exciting opportunity for innovation. She gathered her team for a brainstorming session, welcoming all ideas—no matter how unconventional. Together, they developed a new line of eco-friendly products aligned with the evolving preferences of their customer base. This agile pivot not only saved the company from potential losses but also positioned them as industry leaders in sustainability.

In another example, take the case of Carlos, a tech executive overseeing a team developing a new software application. Early in the development phase, the team encountered significant setbacks due to changing requirements from their clients. Rather than clinging to the original timeline, Carlos exemplified adaptive leadership by facilitating an open dialogue with his team. He prioritized understanding their struggles and encouraged them to discuss potential solutions.

Carlos's leadership style resulted in the implementation of agile methodologies, allowing the team to work in short sprints and quickly pivot based on client feedback. This adaptability ultimately delivered a more robust product that exceeded client expectations.

Through these testimonials, we see how agile leadership can manifest in both mindset and methodologies. Agility entails not only the flexibility to adapt strategies but also the courage to embrace change as a constant presence.

Moreover, the importance of agility is amplified in an increasingly uncertain and complex world. The pace of technological advancement, shifting market demands, and global challenges require leaders to be proactive rather than reactive. The organizations that thrive are those where leaders see change as an integral part of their journey, instilling this perspective within their teams.

As organizations pursue agility, they must also be mindful of the pitfalls that can hinder their progress. One common mistake is the tendency to confuse agility with an absence of structure. While agility promotes flexibility, it does not imply a lack of organization. Effective agile leaders understand the importance of establishing clear goals and frameworks that guide decision-making while allowing for adaptability.

Furthermore, leaders who genuinely embrace agility must overcome resistance to change, particularly from individuals who may prefer the comfort of familiar routines. Leaders should proactively engage these individuals, addressing their concerns and demonstrating the tangible benefits of a culture of agility—a willingness to pivot swiftly can lead to enhanced outcomes for everyone involved.

A culture of agility extends beyond individual leaders and permeates the entire organization. It requires collective commitment and active engagement at every level. Leaders can build this culture by implementing training programs focused on developing agile mindsets and skills. Workshops, mentorship, and cross-functional collaboration encourage collective learning and reinforce the organization's commitment to agility.

Additionally, organizations must celebrate agility by recognizing and rewarding behaviors that demonstrate adaptability. When leaders publicly acknowledge team members who have exhibited agility, they reinforce the notion that such qualities are not only valued but expected. This positive reinforcement fosters a sense of community where everyone feels empowered to participate in the journey towards a more agile organization.

The significance of being agile and adaptable in leadership roles cannot be overstated. The world continues to change rapidly, with unprecedented challenges and exciting opportunities on the horizon. An organization that fosters a culture of agility is better equipped to navigate these shifts and emerge stronger than before. However, it requires commitment, courage, and a strong sense of community.

As leaders reflect on their own journeys and the attributes that define them, embracing a culture of agility represents a profound shift in perspective. It calls for a recognition that the pursuit of perfection is a fleeting and often unattainable goal. Instead, leaders should champion progress—a continuous journey characterized by growth, learning, and adaptation.

In conclusion, leaders today must embrace change as an essential component of their identity. Cognitive frameworks, such as growth mindset and adaptive leadership, provide invaluable tools for navigating uncertainty. Through powerful testimonials from contemporary leaders, we see how agility can inspire innovation, enhance collaboration, and drive success in the face of adversity. As organizations continue to evolve, it is the culture of agility that will empower them to thrive in a dynamic world.

Leading by Example

In the realm of leadership, few things are more powerful than leading by example. The ability of leaders to embody the values they espouse can create an environment where those values thrive and encourage collective growth. This subchapter will delve deeply into how leaders who prioritize humility and openness to feedback not only enhance their own effectiveness but also cultivate these qualities in their teams. By sharing real-life stories of leaders who have successfully navigated their journeys with a focus on progress rather than perfection, we will highlight the transformative effects of leading by example.

One of the most notable stories that illustrate this concept is that of Angela, a CEO of a mid-sized tech company in Silicon Valley. Angela had a stellar background, having worked her way up through the ranks from a software engineer to an executive role. Her success, however, was not just attributed to her technical skills or her sharp business acumen; rather, it was her ability to come across as relatable and approachable that set her apart.

From her first days in the corner office, Angela made it a point to showcase her belief in continuous learning and humility. Every week, she held an open forum where team members, from interns to senior executives, could share their ideas and insights without fear of judgment. One particularly memorable session occurred when a novice software developer suggested a modification to the company's flagship product. Rather than dismissing the suggestion, Angela invited the developer to present it to the larger team. The proposal sparked a thorough discussion, leading to refinements of the original idea and ultimately improving the product significantly.

Angela's willingness to admit that she could learn from anyone in the organization set a potent precedent. Employees felt encouraged to share their own perspectives without holding back, knowing that their voices mattered. The culture of openness cultivated by Angela allowed the company to innovate continuously and stay ahead of market trends. When leaders show vulnerability, it lifts the veil of perfectionism that often permeates corporate environments. Angela's experience is a vivid example of how humility not only enhances a leader's credibility but also fosters an atmosphere where progress becomes a collective goal, not merely an individual achievement.

Another compelling narrative comes from the world of sports, specifically the story of a professional basketball coach named Marcus. When Marcus took the helm of a struggling team, he understood that turning the team's fortunes around would require more than just strategic planning; it would require a cultural shift. With a history of success in other teams, he recognized that humility must underpin his coaching philosophy if he wished to inspire change.

In one of his initial team meetings, Marcus laid down the foundation of his leadership style. Instead of focusing solely on winning games, he emphasized the importance of growth, effort, and learning from failures. After a particularly rough tournament where the team lost several critical games, Marcus gathered the players for a candid discussion. He shared his own experiences of failure—how he had missed critical game-winning shots in his earlier career and how he learned far more from his losses than from his victories. His poignant storytelling provided the players with a sense of solidarity and encouraged them to reflect openly on their own mistakes.

By sharing his vulnerabilities, Marcus created a safe space where players could discuss their own performances, seek feedback, and develop strategies for improvement. As a result, the culture within the team shifted from one that shunned mistakes to one that embraced them. The players began to hold each other accountable, offering not just criticism but constructive advice rooted in a shared understanding of their collective struggles. The transformation was remarkable. By prioritizing progress over perfection, Marcus led the team not only to a championship victory eventually but also to a newfound camaraderie that extended far beyond the court.

A more corporate example can be drawn from a leader named Rahul, who was the Chief Financial Officer of a multinational corporation. Known for his analytical prowess, many were surprised when he decided to introduce a new performance review process that deviated from the standard model of quantifying performance based on metrics and profits. Instead, Rahul sought to incorporate qualitative feedback into the reviews, focusing on employees' growth and areas for improvement.

As he rolled out this initiative, Rahul led by example. He volunteered to be the first to undergo this new review process, inviting his colleagues to assess his performance based on the criteria he was setting for everyone else. In his review, he openly acknowledged areas where he had faltered and how he intended to enhance his skills. This act of transparency did not just win him respect; it cultivated a sense of trust and mutual accountability among his peers.

Team members reported feeling more valued and heard through this new process, leading to a revitalized workplace environment. The culture shifted to one where it became acceptable to discuss setbacks openly, and even leaders found themselves more receptive to feedback. This practice caused a cascading effect throughout the organization, eventually leading to increased employee retention and overall satisfaction. Rahul's example underscores how embodying humility can redefine expectations and stimulate positive change — creating a culture that fuels growth rather than stifles it.

Now let's explore the poignant journey of Lisa, a nonprofit organization director dedicated to environmental conservation. Upon taking leadership, Lisa discovered that although the organization had a dedicated team, they lacked enthusiasm and innovation. In her initial assessments, she found that members were hesitant to share their ideas due to a fear of rejection from prior leadership styles that had favored a top-down approach.

Determined to activate the potential of her team, Lisa hosted a brainstorming retreat that focused not only on generating innovative strategies but also on fostering trust. Before this meeting, she shared her own missteps in previous projects, discussing what she learned from each failure and how it reshaped her approach to leadership. In this retreat, Lisa emphasized her belief in progress by asking each team member to voice one idea and one mistake. This structure allowed for collective reflection and mutual support, paving the way for an open exchange of ideas.

What emerged from that retreat was nothing short of remarkable. Team members began to share outlandish ideas—proposals they previously thought too radical to propose. One member suggested a local outreach program that culminated in a city-wide cleanup, which became one of the nonprofit's most successful initiatives over the coming years. Lisa's commitment to humility set a tone that transformed fear into inspiration. As team members began to see their contributions valued and recognized, they bonded over shared successes and challenges, driving the organization toward impactful progress.

The significance of leading by example in cultivating humility and openness extends beyond individual narratives. Research supports the notion that leaders who embody these qualities can significantly improve organizational dynamics. A study published in the Harvard Business Review reveals that teams led by humble leaders are more likely to engage in knowledge sharing, which is critical for innovation. When leaders demonstrate a willingness to learn from their team, it encourages reciprocal behaviors and creates a learning culture. It becomes evident that the context of humility has impactful ripples that extend throughout the organization, fostering an environment where learning is normalized.

In another compelling study, researchers found that when employees perceive their leaders as open to feedback, they report higher job satisfaction and improved morale. Such findings correlate tightly with organizations' overall performance. When leaders prioritize their learning journey alongside their teams, they disrupt the detrimental cycle of perfectionism, which often stymies creativity and risk-taking. As discussions shift toward progress, flexibility in approach gains centrality, allowing teams to pivot and adapt without fear of failure.

While sharing stories and research, it is equally paramount to acknowledge that embodying humility and openness is not a seamless journey. Leaders will inevitably face moments of doubt and challenges, perhaps needing to reassess their approaches continually. Embracing these challenges openly can be an additional lesson in leading by example. The willingness to scck hclp and ask for feedback, even in leadership roles, demonstrates that vulnerability does not equate to weakness; rather, it strengthens the fabric of team alliance.

In our exploration of leaders embodying humility and openness, we see a mosaic of experiences paving the path to progress. Each story shared emphasizes the significance of collective growth, where recognition of mistakes and accountability drives inclusivity and innovation. These stories not only inspire current leaders but also serve as a powerful reminder for aspiring leaders that perfection is a mirage. In claiming our imperfections, we foster environments ripe for authenticity, creativity, and genuine collaboration.

To sum up, leading by example is a compelling strategy that all leaders should prioritize. Angela, Marcus, Rahul, and Lisa demonstrate that humility and openness yield transformative results for both leaders and their teams. Such qualities diffuse the myths of ideal leadership, breaking the barrier of perfectionism and enabling organizations to thrive through enhanced collaboration and creativity. This cultural shift honoring progress over perfection is the blueprint for a resilient leadership model capable of navigating the complexities of today's dynamic environments. As leaders embrace the journey of continuous learning and openness, they cultivate the very values that propel their teams and organizations toward sustainable growth and success.

CHAPTER EIGHT

CREATING A LEADERSHIP PLAYBOOK

Synthesizing Insights

The essence of effective leadership doesn't solely lie in possessing innate traits or charisma. Rather, it emerges from a harmonious blend of fundamental principles, cultivated through experience and introspection. In this subchapter, we will synthesize the insights gathered from previous chapters, forming a cohesive framework that leaders can employ and tailor to their unique organizational contexts. This is not merely an academic exercise; it is a call to action—to reconsider, refine, and reinvigorate your approach to leadership with actionable strategies.

To create a successful leadership playbook, we begin by grounding our framework in the core principles discussed throughout this book: the balancing act between tolerance and pride, the elevation of constructive conflict, the acknowledgement of fallibility, and the pursuit of sustainable change. By interweaving these concepts, we can establish a roadmap that guides leaders toward impactful and meaningful leadership.

A. Understanding the Core Principles

1. **The Interplay of Tolerance and Pride**

The journey of leadership is often a paradoxical one where tolerance and pride must coexist. On one hand, leaders are tasked with embracing diverse perspectives, fostering an inclusive environment where every voice is valued. On the other, they must carry a sense of pride in their missions, instilling confidence in their teams to achieve excellence. The insight here is the recognition that tolerating differing opinions is not synonymous with capitulating to mediocrity. Instead, it involves actively engaging in challenging discussions, recognizing the importance of conflict as a catalyst for creativity and innovation.

Leaders must harness the power of both qualities, ensuring that pride does not tip into arrogance and that tolerance does not devolve into complacency.

2. **Embracing Constructive Conflict**

Conflict, when approached constructively, holds the potential to catalyze growth and innovation. The leaders who have harnessed the power of conflict understand that it is an essential ingredient in fostering collaboration. They encourage open dialogue, creating safe spaces where team members feel empowered to express dissent and challenge ideas. The insights from the narratives shared in the previous chapters illustrate how constructive conflict can lead to breakthrough solutions and enhance team dynamics.

A crucial strategy for leaders is to redefine their relationship with conflict, acknowledging it as an ally rather than an adversary. This shift requires ongoing training, coaching, and reinforcement of the value of diverse perspectives in driving progress.

3. **Acknowledging the Fallibility of Leaders**

The best leaders understand that they are not infallible. Acknowledging one's flaws and vulnerabilities fosters an environment where everyone feels safe to learn from mistakes. The stories shared in previous chapters reveal that the most revered leaders are those willing to admit when they are wrong and to accept feedback without defensiveness.

This insight can be operationalized through practices that encourage humility and openness to learning. Leaders should implement regular reflection sessions, feedback protocols, and candid discussions about failures and missteps—both team-wide and individually.

4. **Pursuing Sustainable Change**

Change is an inevitable aspect of any organization's lifecycle. The successful leaders of our time are those who not only embrace change but celebrate its transformative power. Sustainable change does not occur through periodic adjustments; rather, it requires a mindset that prioritizes agility and adaptability.

Effective change strategies include mechanisms for continuous improvement, where the focus remains on forward momentum and the integration of new ideas. Leadership teams should regularly review their strategic goals, assess the internal and external environments, and pivot as necessary.

B. Crafting the Leadership Framework

Having established the core principles of effective leadership, we can now synthesize these insights into a coherent framework to enhance leadership practices. This framework consists of interrelated components that support one another, culminating in a comprehensive strategy to develop resilient and adaptive leaders.

1. **Establishing Vision and Values**

The foundation of impactful leadership is clarity of vision and alignment of values. Every leader must articulate a clear vision that resonates with their team members, effectively communicating the goals and aspirations of the organization. This vision should be articulated in a way that invites collaboration and participation from all team members, fostering a sense of ownership and commitment.

Equally important is the establishment of core organizational values that guide behavior and decision-making processes. Values should encompass notions of respect, integrity, agility, and innovation—each serving as a touchstone for evaluating actions and choices across the organization.

2. **Cultivating a Culture of Openness and Feedback**

Leaders must prioritize the establishment of a feedback-rich culture. This can be facilitated through regular check-ins, anonymous feedback mechanisms, and open forums where employees can voice their thoughts and opinions. A culture that values feedback allows teams to thrive, as it encourages transparent communication, collaboration, and continuous learning.

To implement this, consider developing structured feedback cycles that encompass both upward and downward feedback across the organizational hierarchy. Beyond evaluations, encourage informal feedback loops through catch-up meetings or team-building activities. Make sure leaders model what it means to receive feedback openly and to act upon it constructively.

3. **Training for Conflict Management**

As discussed, conflict is a crucial aspect of organizational life. Thus, training programs should incorporate modules focused on conflict resolution and constructive communication. These initiatives can equip leaders and team members with skills necessary to navigate difficult conversations and disagreements without damaging relationships.

Develop role-playing scenarios where team members practice handling various conflicts, providing them with tangible strategies for resolution. Invite external experts to facilitate workshops that delve into advanced negotiation techniques, underscoring the idea that conflict can stimulate creativity and innovation rather than perpetuate division.

4. **Encouraging Accountability and Humility**

1. **Building Ownership**

An essential element of leadership is accountability. Successful leaders unequivocally embrace accountability at both personal and organizational levels. Build mechanisms that incorporate accountability through setting clear expectations and ensuring individuals are responsible for their roles and outputs. This means measuring not only results but also the processes that lead to those results.

2. **Cultivating Humility**

Leaders must exemplify humility by actively seeking input from others, acknowledging the contributions of their team members, and engaging in transparent decision-making processes. Regular reflections, such as team retrospectives, can serve as powerful tools for fostering an environment of shared learning.

5. **Embedding Agility in Leadership Practices**

Given the unpredictable nature of today's business landscape, prioritizing agility becomes paramount. To build this agility, ensure leaders are equipped with the skills and tools to pivot as circumstances change. Encourage experimentation and innovation in processes, allowing teams to adapt their strategies in real time.

Consider creating cross-functional teams to address various challenges, granting members the authority to experiment with solutions without bureaucratic hindrances. Promote the idea that failure is a natural part of the process and should be viewed as an opportunity for learning, not as a setback.

C. Implementing the Framework in Real-World Scenarios

With the framework established, it's essential to contextualize its application through real-world scenarios demonstrating how leaders can integrate these strategies into their daily operations. Below are examples of how each component of the framework can be brought to life:

1. **Vision and Values in Action**

Consider a technology startup aiming to disrupt the educational sector. The CEO articulates a vision to reshape learning experiences globally by leveraging technology. Each team member participates in a workshop to develop a shared set of core values: innovation, inclusivity, and collaboration. As the organization grows, the team continually refers back to this vision, ensuring initiatives align with their overarching purpose.

2. **Culture of Openness and Feedback**

In a large consulting firm, the leadership introduced bi-weekly feedback forums where consultants share their experiences and challenges openly. The firm's culture values every opinion as essential to growth, making feedback a cornerstone of decision-making. As a result, employee satisfaction improves markedly, and teams collaborate more effectively on projects.

3. **Conflict Management Training**

A healthcare organization identifies communication issues around patient care. Executives initiate a conflict resolution training program for staff, encouraging role-playing scenarios focused on interdepartmental communication challenges. This proactive approach not only enhances collaboration but also leads to improved patient outcomes, as barriers to information flow dissolve.

4. **Accountability and Humility**

In a manufacturing company, plant managers implement a peer review system where teams regularly present their performance metrics and receive constructive feedback from their peers. This initiative fosters ownership and reinforces a culture of learning, leading to enhanced operational efficiency.

5. **Agility in Practice**

Amid a market shift, a retail chain opts to create small, nimble teams focused on rapid testing of new initiatives. The leaders empower these teams to explore new product lines with minimal oversight, alongside regular reviews to assess their impact. This approach enables the organization to stay relevant and responsive to consumer demands effectively.

D. Measuring Progress and Impact

As leaders implement the synthesized insights presented in this playbook, it is vital to measure progress and impact continually. This occurs not only through evaluation metrics but also through qualitative assessments of team dynamics and morale.

1. **Setting Metrics for Success**

Establish clear KPIs (Key Performance Indicators) related to the changes implemented. This may include measuring engagement scores, satisfaction ratings, turnover rates, and productivity metrics. Additionally, qualitative metrics such as employee testimonials can provide deeper insights into cultural shifts.

2. **Conducting Regular Assessments**

Plan routine evaluations of the framework's effectiveness, reviewing how well the core principles are being embraced within the organization. Leaders should gather feedback through pulse surveys, focus groups, or interviews. This continuous feedback loop allows leaders to make necessary adjustments while celebrating successes and reinforcing growth.

3. **Iterative Refinement**

Finally, leaders must embrace the notion of iterative refinement. As the organization evolves and external conditions shift, the playbook should be revisited and adapted. An organization's ability to pivot and refine its framework will be crucial in ensuring long-term success.

E. Conclusion

In synthesizing the insights from previous chapters, we have developed a practical leadership framework rooted in adaptability, humility, and collaborative growth. The strategies outlined empower leaders to foster an organizational culture that values diverse perspectives, embraces conflict as a catalyst for innovation, acknowledges fallibility as an opportunity for learning, and pursues sustainable change.

By committing to this leadership playbook, readers will position themselves as resilient leaders equipped to face the challenges of modern organizational life. The path ahead may not be easy, but the rewards of cultivating an environment where leaders and teams thrive together will undeniably lead to transformative results. Through the lens of humility, courage, and an unwavering commitment to progress, leaders can embrace their roles as stewards of change, ensuring their organizations remain agile and prepared for the future.

The Fundamentals of Resilient Leadership

In today's rapidly changing organizational landscape, the need for resilient leadership has never been more pronounced. Organizations must navigate a complex array of challenges, from technological disruptions to changing consumer expectations, while simultaneously fostering a culture that empowers and motivates teams. At the heart of resilient leadership lies a core set of traits and practices that enable leaders not just to survive but to thrive amid volatility and uncertainty. In this subchapter, we will explore the fundamental characteristics of resilient leadership, focusing particularly on emotional intelligence, openness to feedback, and a steadfast commitment to team development.

Emotional intelligence, often referred to as EQ, is a critical component of resilient leadership. While traditional leadership models may have prioritized technical skills or cognitive intelligence, contemporary research indicates that emotional intelligence plays a decisive role in effective leadership. At its core, emotional intelligence encompasses the ability to perceive, understand, and manage emotions—both one's own and those of others.

Leaders with high emotional intelligence can read the emotional climate of their teams, recognizing stress levels, morale, and motivation. This capacity enhances their ability to respond effectively during times of crisis or change. For instance, consider a leader who notices increased anxiety within their team due to an impending organizational restructure. Rather than avoiding the subject or glossing over team concerns, a resilient leader engages in open dialogue, addressing fears and providing reassurance. This not only fosters trust but also strengthens team cohesion and morale.

Effective communication also plays a crucial role in the exercise of emotional intelligence. Leaders should cultivate an environment where team members feel safe expressing their thoughts and emotions. Using active listening techniques—such as summarizing what a team member has said, asking clarifying questions, or reflecting feelings—signals to the team that their input is valued. This validation is vital during challenging times when team members may feel vulnerable or uncertain.

Furthermore, resilient leaders leverage emotional intelligence to manage their own responses to stress and adversity. They develop self-awareness, recognizing their emotions and how these feelings may influence their decision-making and interaction with others. By practicing self-regulation, these leaders can maintain composure, adaptability, and flexibility, which are essential when navigating complex or high-pressure situations.

The ability to empathize with team members ensures that leaders can provide the support needed during turbulent times. Empathy is the cornerstone of building strong interpersonal relationships, allowing leaders to connect with team members at a deeper level. When employees feel understood and valued, they are more likely to contribute positively to the organizational culture, even amidst challenges.

Transitioning from emotional intelligence, we now focus on the significance of openness to feedback as another fundamental of resilient leadership. In a dynamic environment, feedback acts as a guide, providing insights into how effectively leaders are meeting the needs of their teams. However, many leaders struggle to embrace feedback due to the fear of criticism or a desire to maintain a strong public image.

Resilient leaders reframe feedback as an essential tool for growth rather than a negative reflection of their capabilities. They actively solicit feedback from their teams and view it as an opportunity to learn and improve. This practice creates a culture of continuous development and reinforces the understanding that no one has all the answers. A leader's willingness to openly receive feedback also encourages team members to voice their thoughts and suggestions, ensuring a rich exchange of ideas and perspectives.

Establishing regular feedback mechanisms, such as one-on-one check-ins or anonymous surveys, helps to normalize the practice while enhancing its effectiveness. Moreover, leaders who model this behavior can set a precedent for their teams, fostering an environment where feedback is seen as a positive, integral part of the working culture rather than a punitive measure.

It is equally important for leaders to demonstrate humility in the feedback process. Recognizing one's imperfections and areas for growth creates an authentic leadership style that resonates with team members. Resilient leaders share their learning journeys, articulating how they've used feedback to adjust their leadership styles or address challenges. This transparency not only builds trust but also shows that growth is a lifelong endeavor, one that transcends rank or title.

A commitment to team development, another cornerstone of resilient leadership, encapsulates the investment in a team's growth, skills enhancement, and overall well-being. Resilient leaders understand that their success is intertwined with the success of their teams. Therefore, they prioritize creating opportunities for professional and personal development, fostering an environment where learning is encouraged and celebrated.

The first step in fostering team development involves investing time in understanding the unique strengths and weaknesses of each team member. This understanding allows leaders to tailor development opportunities that align with both individual aspirations and organizational goals. For example, a leader may identify that a team member exhibits strong analytical skills but lacks confidence in public speaking. By encouraging that employee to participate in training or present at team meetings, the leader helps bolster their confidence while enhancing overall team competence.

Moreover, resilient leaders recognize the importance of mentorship and coaching. Providing regular support and guidance not only boosts individual performance but also reinforces a culture of collaboration and knowledge-sharing within the team. These developmental interactions can take many forms, from casual conversations to structured mentorship programs. The investment of time and energy speaks volumes about a leader's commitment to their team's success.

Creating a safe space for team members to engage in skill-sharing enhances the collective competency and adaptability of the group. Resilient leaders encourage collaborative learning, where team members can share their expertise and learn from one another. This approach not only develops individual skills but also strengthens relationships among team members, creating a sense of unity and shared purpose.

Furthermore, celebrating successes—both big and small—plays a crucial role in team development. Resilient leaders take time to acknowledge achievements, instilling a sense of pride in both individual and collective efforts. Recognition can take various forms, from public praise in meetings to private notes of appreciation. Acknowledging hard work fosters motivation and inspires team members to continue striving for excellence.

In this regard, resilient leaders are often seen as coaches rather than mere supervisors. They empower their teams by providing the necessary resources, guidance, and encouragement to take ownership of their work. This transitional shift in leadership style often results in amplified levels of engagement, creativity, and problem-solving capabilities throughout the organization.

Ultimately, resilient leadership hinges on building a robust foundation of emotional intelligence, an openness to feedback, and a dedicated commitment to team development. Leaders who embody these traits instill a sense of purpose and cohesiveness within their teams, driving them toward success in the face of adversity.

As we analyze these characteristics further, it becomes increasingly evident that resilient leaders are not born with these qualities; rather, they are cultivated through conscious practice and self-reflection. Engaging in self-assessment and seeking out opportunities for development allows leaders to hone their skills continuously.

Regularly reflecting on one's leadership style through journaling or discussion groups with peers can enhance self-awareness. Recognizing patterns, strengths, weaknesses, and opportunities for growth is essential for becoming a more effective and resilient leader.

To further cultivate resilience, leaders might consider engaging in training and development programs focused on emotional intelligence, feedback mechanisms, and team dynamics. Many organizations offer workshops, seminars, and resources aimed at helping leaders strengthen these vital characteristics. Participating in these initiatives signals a commitment to personal growth and the betterment of the organization as a whole.

Collaboration with mentors who exemplify resilience provides enriching insights into effective leadership practices. Learning from others' experiences often sheds light on unique strategies and philosophies that can be integrated into one's leadership approach. Regardless of the context, mentorship serves as a powerful catalyst for growth and change.

Driving change is a significant aspect of resilient leadership, but it requires both courage and compassion. Leaders should actively embrace their roles as change agents, understanding that employee buy-in is essential for successful transitions. The way leaders frame changes can profoundly influence how teams react and adapt. Rather than dictating change from the top down, resilient leaders should engage their teams in various stages of the decision-making process.

A collaborative approach to change enhances ownership and accountability among team members, who are far more likely to embrace transitions when they feel included in the conversation. Creating forums for discussion and brainstorming allows for diverse perspectives to be shared, giving leaders richer insights into potential ramifications of changes and how they may impact the organization.

In this dynamic process, it is essential for leaders to communicate clearly the rationale behind changes while addressing potential challenges openly. The transparency in discussion builds trust, allowing teams to feel more secure in navigating uncertain futures together.

Throughout this journey of cultivating resilience, we must acknowledge that leaders are just as susceptible to setbacks and stress as any team member. Maintaining one's well-being during tumultuous times requires intentionality and prioritization. Resilient leaders model self-care practices, whether through regular exercise, mindfulness techniques, or adequate time off.

By demonstrating the importance of balance and self-care, leaders empower their teams to prioritize their well-being as well. Encouragement to take time for themselves enhances overall performance, as well-rested, healthy individuals can contribute positively to the organization.

To encapsulate, the fundamentals of resilient leadership are intertwined with emotional intelligence, openness to feedback, and a commitment to team development. Leaders who embrace these characteristics will find themselves better equipped to face adversity head-on, while driving positive change within their organizations. As we navigate the complexities of the modern workplace, it is crucial to prioritize these traits not only as individual attributes but as essential components of organizational culture.

In an era characterized by uncertainty, the demand for resilient leadership is greater than ever. Leaders equipped with emotional intelligence, feedback receptivity, and dedication to team development will not only weather adversity but will inspire their teams to do the same, fostering a culture where resilience transforms challenges into opportunities for growth. The journey toward becoming a resilient leader is one of continual development, a commitment to self-improvement, and a steadfast belief in the power of collaboration and growth.

As we further explore the creation of a leadership playbook, let us remember that resilience is not merely a goal; it is a guiding principle that informs all aspects of effective leadership. By embedding emotional intelligence, openness to feedback, and team development at the core of our leadership practices, we set the stage for success in an ever-evolving world.

A Guiding Manual for Future Leaders

In the rapidly evolving landscape of leadership, the journey towards becoming an effective leader transcends the traditional notions of authority and command. It requires a commitment to continuous self-improvement, adaptability, and a deep understanding of the people you lead. This manual aims to equip future leaders with hands-on insights that foster growth, resilience, and the ability to inspire teams amid ongoing change.

1. Defining Your Leadership Philosophy

Every leader must start with a personal leadership philosophy. This guiding principle serves as the foundation for your approach to leadership, influencing your decisions, behaviors, and interactions with team members. To articulate your leadership philosophy:

- Reflect on your values and experiences. Ask yourself what matters most to you in leadership. Is it integrity? Innovation? Empowerment?

- Consider how these values shape your vision of effective leadership.

- Write a concise statement that embodies your philosophy. Share this with your team to foster transparency and alignment.

2. Embracing Emotional Intelligence

Emotional intelligence (EQ) is essential for effective leadership. High EQ enables leaders to connect with their teams on a deeper level, making it easier to motivate and inspire. To enhance your emotional intelligence:

- Practice self-awareness: Regularly assess your emotions and how they affect your behavior. Journaling can help you recognize patterns.

- Develop empathy: Engage actively with your employees, listening to their concerns and understanding their perspectives without judgment.

- Utilize social skills: Foster relationships by being approachable, demonstrating concern for your team's well-being, and effectively managing conflict through communication.

3. Prioritizing Continuous Learning

In today's fast-paced world, leaders must cultivate a habit of continuous learning. This enables you to stay abreast of industry trends and sharpen your leadership skills. Here are ways to prioritize learning:

- Set a personal growth plan: Identify areas where you wish to develop and allocate time to learn about those topics.

- Seek mentorship: Connect with experienced leaders who can provide guidance, share insights, and offer constructive feedback on your leadership approach.

- Encourage a culture of learning within your team: Promote professional development opportunities and provide resources for your team members to grow alongside you.

4. Conducting Regular Self-Assessments

Self-assessment is crucial for effective leadership. It allows you to gauge your effectiveness and identify areas for improvement. Incorporate self-assessment into your regular routine:

- Utilize feedback: Collect feedback through surveys or informal check-ins with your team to understand their perception of your leadership.

- Reflect on successes and failures: Maintain a leadership journal highlighting key victories and challenges. Analyze what contributed to these outcomes and what changes you might make moving forward.

- Set specific goals: Use insights from your reflections to set measurable and actionable leadership goals for the coming months.

5. Implementing Constructive Feedback Loops

Feedback is a two-way street. As a leader, you should encourage open communication where team members feel comfortable sharing their thoughts and ideas. Here's how:

- Foster a safe environment: Make it clear that you value input and won't react defensively to constructive criticism.

- Regularly solicit feedback: Schedule one-on-one meetings or team discussions aimed solely at gathering insights on your leadership style and decisions.

- Act on the feedback: Show your team that you take their input seriously by implementing changes when feasible. Acknowledging their contribution builds trust and respect.

6. Cultivating an Inclusive Culture

Diversity and inclusion are foundational to modern leadership. Actively cultivating an inclusive culture broadens the perspectives within your team and promotes innovation. Steps to ensure inclusion include:

- Assess diversity metrics: Review the makeup of your team and identify areas needing improvement in diversity.

- Implement inclusive policies: Ensure hiring practices and workplace policies encourage diverse candidates and support their growth.

- Celebrate diversity: Acknowledge and celebrate the unique contributions of each team member, fostering a sense of belonging.

7. Promoting Team Engagement

Engaged teams are more productive and committed. To promote engagement:

- Encourage autonomy: Empower your team members by delegating responsibilities that align with their skills and interests, fostering ownership of their work.

- Recognize achievements: Celebrate individual and team accomplishments—both big and small. Recognition can significantly enhance motivation and morale.

- Facilitate team bonding: Organize team-building activities, both in-person and virtual, to strengthen relationships and enhance collaboration.

8. Addressing Conflict Proactively

Conflict is a natural part of any team dynamic. How you address it defines your leadership effectiveness. To navigate conflict:

- Embrace conflict resolution: View conflict as an opportunity for growth and improvement. Approach issues with an open mind and encourage dialogue among team members.

- Practice active listening: Allow all parties to express their viewpoints fully. Listening actively can reduce tensions and clear misunderstandings.

- Seek win-win outcomes: Aim for solutions that satisfy both party's needs, reinforcing collaboration and trust.

9. Adapting to Change

In an ever-changing business environment, adaptability is paramount for leaders. To enhance adaptability:

- Embrace flexibility: Be willing to pivot your strategy based on new information or shifting circumstances.

- Encourage innovation: Create a culture where team members feel inspired to experiment with new ideas and embrace calculated risks.

- Stay informed: Regularly engage with industry news and trends to anticipate and respond to changes proactively.

10. Leading by Example

As a leader, your actions set the tone for your team. To lead by example:

- Model behavior: Demonstrate the values and work ethic you expect from your team. This builds credibility and respect.

- Share your journey: Be open about your experiences, including successes and struggles. Authenticity resonates with team members and fosters connection.

- Show commitment: Exhibit dedication to the team's goals, consistently prioritizing their interests and development.

Conclusion: The Ongoing Journey of Leadership

This manual serves as your springboard into the world of effective leadership. The strategies outlined are not mere checklists but core values that require nurturing through commitment and self-reflection.

As you embark on this leadership journey, keep the concept of adaptive leadership at the forefront of your mind. The most impactful leaders evolve over time, responding to feedback and external realities while embodying the essential qualities of empathy, humility, and resilience. Your commitment to growth will not only make you a better leader but also create a positive ripple effect on your team and organization as a whole. Embrace the journey, and let it shape you into the leader you are destined to become.

Voices of Change: Real Stories

Leaders' Transformative Journeys

In the ever-evolving landscape of leadership, the journey of each leader is distinct yet universally profound. As we delve into the transformative journeys of several exemplary leaders, we uncover insights that echo the themes of pride and tolerance. These narratives not only illustrate the balance between these two traits but also the vulnerabilities that leaders encounter along the way.

The Journey of Emma Torres

Emma Torres, the CEO of a mid-sized tech firm, found her professional path fraught with challenges that tested her resolve. Initially hailed for her sharp decision-making skills and confidence, Emma faced a particularly turbulent period during her company's significant restructuring phase.

As the chosen leader of change, she felt the pressure of pride pushing her to showcase her unwavering strength. However, she soon realized that the very traits that had served her well could become liabilities when exploited to excess.

During the restructuring process, Emma encountered dissent within her leadership team. Many voices rose against the proposed changes, fearing that the significant layoffs would damage the company's culture and morale. Emma instinctively reacted by asserting her executive authority, pushing back against dissent with fierce pride in her vision for the company's future. She silenced the objections and pressed forward with the restructuring, determined to prove her rationale.

Yet, as the months progressed, Emma noticed a troubling trend—team morale plummeted, and productivity stagnated. The realization struck her: rather than fostering an inclusive culture that welcomed debate and dissent, her leadership had cultivated a climate of fear. The company was becoming a shadow of its former self, floundering under the weight of its own pride.

One fateful afternoon, an employee initiative aimed at reviving team spirit was hijacked by a frank discussion about the ongoing discontent. Emma found herself at the meeting, listening to poignant stories of fear, loss, and frustration. The vulnerability displayed by her team members was a stark contrast to her own armor of pride. It was a raw moment that prompted Emma to take a hard look in the mirror.

Instead of reacting defensively, she took the courageous step of acknowledging her missteps, inviting honest conversation about the community they were building. This pivotal moment marked a turning point in her tenure as a leader. By setting aside her pride and embracing vulnerability, she promoted an environment that welcomed feedback, sparking healing conversations within her team.

As these lines of communication opened, Emma recognized that tolerance in leadership isn't about overlooking issues for the sake of harmony but embracing conflict to promote constructive dialogue. She sought out other leaders who had faced similar challenges and crafted development plans that encouraged her team to voice their concerns openly.

Within six months, Emma transformed her leadership approach by incorporating regular feedback loops into her company's culture. These forums not only allowed individuals to speak candidly, but they also reconstructed the broken trust her actions had eroded. Gradually, the company found its voice, its spirit ignited. The initiatives born from these conversations propelled the company toward innovative solutions, demonstrating how the balance of pride and tolerance, blended with the power of vulnerability, could foster change.

The Journey of Malik Richards

Malik Richards, a prominent community organizer turned city council member, offers another perspective on the complicated dance between pride and tolerance. For Malik, the drive to make a difference was coupled with an innate pride in his roots and the community he represented. He often spoke with passionate conviction about the need for systemic change, which resonated deeply with his constituents.

However, it was during the council's discussions on a monumental policy reform aimed at addressing housing inequality that Malik's journey unveiled the complexities of his leadership role. His pride in advocating for the community often clouded his ability to listen to dissenting views. During several meetings, he was quick to challenge opponents of his vision, inadvertently shutting down essential discussions that would have contributed to more nuanced policy-making.

One night, following a particularly charged council meeting, Malik received feedback from constituents who felt unheard and marginalized. It forced him to confront the paradox of his assertiveness. Instead of embracing the feedback as a springboard for growth, he initially recoiled. Did he want to be a leader that thrived on applause, or one that fostered a collective voice?

After weeks of reflection, Malik made a deliberate shift. He began to host listening sessions within the community, inviting divergent opinions not as threats but as opportunities for deeper understanding. During these forums, he welcomed dissenting views, allowing residents from all backgrounds to express their fears and frustrations candidly. The raw emotion of a mother fighting for her children's future or a veteran sharing stories of displacement humanized the statistics.

Over time, these interactions began to reshape Malik's perspective and approach. His pride transformed into a collective pride, bridging gaps previously overlooked. By embracing vulnerability and acknowledging the limits of his own knowledge, he created a participative environment, one where humility was celebrated, leading to policy reforms that were more inclusive and reflective of the community's true needs.

The council's eventual housing reform passed not just as Malik's success, but as a collective victory for the rich tapestry of voices within the community. The experience taught him that genuine leadership requires an openness to vulnerability which, in itself, fosters tolerance.

The Journey of Sarah Jensen

Sarah Jensen, a co-founder of a highly successful marketing agency, was regarded as a creative genius in the industry. Her innovative strategies propelled her company to fortune, and her confidence earned her accolades from peers. While pride in her accomplishments sparked her personal growth, it was entwined with a subtle arrogance that threatened to overshadow her influence.

However, a significant client failure shattered the facade of invincibility surrounding her leadership. The fallout was swift, leading to financial repercussions and a wave of discontent among her employees who felt the brunt of the consequences. Initially resistant to acknowledging her shortcomings, Sarah embodied the traits of a proud leader battling to maintain a reputation that began to crumble around her.

Amid the chaos, a mentor encouraged Sarah to confront her pride and embrace vulnerability. Inspired, she initiated a series of meetings with her team, laying bare the problems that had been allowed to fester. She spoke candidly about her mistakes, actively seeking feedback on how to rebuild trust within the team as well as with clients.

This approach was transformative. Rather than simply presenting a polished front, Sarah shared her own fears, doubts, and aspirations. Her team reciprocated, voicing frustrations and suggestions that had previously been curbed by fear of reprisal or marginalization.

The newfound transparency exposed the importance of vulnerability. Sarah realized that her pride had once silenced innovation from her team, stifling their creativity and growth. Together, they redefined the agency's vision, guiding it back to the innovative roots that had seeded its success.

As the agency worked through the crisis, Sarah began to cultivate a culture rooted in mutual respect and open dialogue. Each team member was granted a stake in the decision-making process, causing creativity to flourish instead of fade. The collaborative spirit reclaimed the agency's potential, leading to fresh strategies and revitalized campaigns that reflected the passion and talent of the entire organization.

Through these collective experiences, Sarah transformed into a leader who embodies vulnerability, willingness to adapt, and a balance of pride that encourages collaboration rather than competition.

These narratives remind us of the deeply human spirit that inhabits leadership. As the journeys of Emma, Malik, and Sarah illustrate, the struggle to find equilibrium between pride and tolerance is a persistent challenge faced by all leaders. Vulnerability stands as a powerful catalyst for change, each leader's story serves as a testament that when leaders embrace this vulnerability, they can catalyze profound transformations within themselves and their organizations.

The courage to share one's failures, to show humility, and to invite the contributions of others not only strengthens the bonds within their teams but fosters a resilient and innovative culture. As we navigate the journeys of these leaders, let us remember to honor our vulnerabilities and embrace the strength that comes from authentic connection and collaboration, for it is in this very space that the most powerful transformations lie.

Lessons from the Trenches

In the landscape of leadership, the path is rarely linear or free of obstacles. The stories that follow shed light on the profound and complex relationship between pride and humility. These narratives come from leaders who have faced substantial challenges, every one of them reflecting the struggles and victories that shape effective, resilient leadership. In sharing their experiences, these leaders illustrate how having the courage to be imperfect allows for growth—not just personally, but within their organizations as well.

One such leader is Helen, a former CEO of a mid-sized tech company that had been thriving during its early years. Under her leadership, the company became a key player in its industry, but a sudden market downturn left it struggling for survival. Helen found herself facing an uphill battle to reinvigorate not just the business, but also the morale of her employees.

In the face of adversity, Helen had to confront the heavy weight of responsibility she felt for her team's welfare. Her initial instinct was to project strength and confidence; after all, she had earned her position through years of hard work and dedication. However, she quickly recognized that this approach was fostering a culture of silence, where employees felt disengaged and fearful to express their concerns. This acknowledgment was the first step toward a pivotal transformation.

Determined to shift the narrative, Helen organized a series of open forums to discuss the company's challenges. It was during these sessions that she learned the invaluable power of vulnerability. She shared candidly about her fears and uncertainties regarding the company's future, admitting that she did not have all the answers. This act of authenticity opened the floodgates of dialogue within her team, allowing employees to voice their worries, suggestions, and innovative ideas to navigate the turmoil. Through this experience, Helen learned that vulnerability was not a sign of weakness but rather a source of strength that fosters trust.

Helen's story exemplifies the intricate balance between pride and humility. Her professional pride as an accomplished leader was put to the test, forcing her to embrace humility in a scenario where she could either choose to maintain authority or promote authenticity. The latter proved more fruitful, allowing her company to pivot and adapt based on the collective input of her team. As a result, morale improved, ideas flourished, and eventually, the company found a new path toward growth.

Similarly, let's turn to the story of Marco, a senior operations manager at a manufacturing plant that faced severe disruptions due to supply chain issues. Marco had built a reputation for being a decisive and efficient leader, often taking pride in his ability to resolve problems swiftly. However, when confronted with the multifaceted nature of the supply chain crisis, he found himself perplexed and overwhelmed.

Rather than doubling down on his usual approach, Marco took a step back and allowed himself to engage his team in problem-solving discussions. He recognized that his reliance on his own past successes was leading him to overlook valuable insights from those around him. By inviting input from his staff, he shifted the focus from his singular perspective to a collective intelligence that empowered the entire team.

During these discussions, an employee named Rachel proposed a creative solution that involved seeking alternative suppliers and diversifying their sourcing strategy. This was a perspective that Marco had not previously considered, showing him the danger of pride that limits creative solutions. By coordinating with Rachel and others, Marco was not only able to address the immediate supply chain issues but also foster a culture of collaboration that would last beyond the crisis.

Both Helen and Marco demonstrate the value of humility in leadership, especially when navigating adversity. Their narratives illustrate how embracing vulnerability can lead to enhanced communication, innovative problem-solving, and the re-establishment of a culture that encourages growth rather than stagnation. These leaders learned that acknowledging their limits created a foundation for collective resilience.

In contrast, consider the experience of Laura, a nonprofit director who encountered resistance from her board while attempting to implement a new strategic initiative. Known for her unwavering confidence, Laura initially approached the board meeting with the same dogged determination that had driven her success in the past. However, this time, the results were starkly different. Pushback and criticism washed over her, leading to tension and frustration.

Realizing that her pride might be blinding her to valuable feedback, Laura took a different approach in subsequent meetings. Rather than arguing her points with fervor, she began to actively listen, soliciting her board's perspectives and concerns. As they voiced their reservations, she learned important lessons about their motivations and feelings, which were deeply rooted in their wisdom and experiences.

This pivot allowed Laura to engage with her board constructively, adapting her proposal to align with their vision. By doing so, she not only salvaged the initiative but also strengthened her relationships with board members, enhancing trust and demonstrating that vulnerability could lead to profound insights. Her journey underscores the importance of balancing pride in one's vision with the humility to adjust in the face of valid criticism.

Now, let's explore the narrative of Tom, a young entrepreneur who founded a startup dedicated to sustainability. Tom was passionate, full of ideas, and natural in his ability to inspire others. However, when his startup began to face financial pressures, he found himself trapped in the confines of his own pride. He resisted reaching out for help, believing he should have the answers and solutions readily available simply due to his leadership role.

Over time, the mounting pressure began to take a toll on Tom, leading to burnout and casting a shadow over his once-vibrant company culture. As he struggled in silence, his team became increasingly disconnected, confused by the shift in his demeanor. It was only after a particularly trying day filled with setbacks that Tom decided to break the silence.

One evening, he called an emergency meeting, gathering his team and laying bare his feelings of inadequacy. This moment marked a pivotal turning point. Rather than shying away from his vulnerabilities, Tom instead chose to lean into them, inviting his team to share their thoughts and suggestions on how to steer the company back to stability.

This act of openness sparked a renewed sense of camaraderie among the team, leading to brainstorming sessions that uncovered untapped potential within the staff. Tom's decision to embrace humility by showcasing his own challenges made the employees feel safe to express their ideas and emotions in return. Ultimately, they devised a plan that not only addressed their financial challenges but also pivoted the startups' focus into a more community-oriented approach, enhancing brand loyalty and support.

These stories collectively emphasize that true leadership is often forged in the fires of adversity. Helen, Marco, Laura, and Tom each discovered that pride, when left unchecked, could blind even the most capable leaders to the potential for collaboration and growth that existed among their teams. Each faced their challenges head-on, but it was only through the embrace of humility and vulnerability that they could forge paths toward recovery and innovation.

Leaders in the trenches of adversity need to remember that it is the lessons learned through the bumps in the road that prepare them for greater responsibilities. Learning to balance pride with humility allows leaders to cultivate environments where individuals feel valued and heard, ultimately fostering creativity and resilience.

In conclusion, stories such as these underscore the importance of resilience amid challenges; they show that embracing vulnerability is not a weakness but an essential ingredient to effective leadership. By prioritizing open communication, acknowledging their imperfections, and engaging their teams, these leaders transformed their respective organizations, instilling a sense of hope, trust, and a renewed vision.

In the face of adversity, it is not the avoidance of challenges but the willingness to confront them, share the burden, and grow that defines great leadership. Aspiring leaders would do well to heed these lessons from the trenches, as they pave the way for a future that is not only successful but also grounded in collective triumphs and shared humanity.

Inspiring Future Generations

In the contemporary world of leadership, the ripple effect of one's actions and values can transcend generations. As we delve into the era of rapid change, leaders today not only bear the responsibilities of guiding their organizations but also have the profound privilege and obligation of shaping the future of leadership itself. This subchapter explores how established leaders—through their stories and experiences—serve as beacons of inspiration for the next generation, empowering emerging leaders to tread confidently on their own paths while remaining rooted in their values.

Every great leader has a legacy, yet the most impactful leaders understand that their legacy isn't merely a collection of professional achievements. It's woven into the lives they have touched, the lessons they have imparted, and the values they have modeled. These leaders recognize that sharing stories from their journeys—both triumphant and tumultuous—acts as a guiding compass for up-and-coming leaders who are navigating their own uncharted territories.

The power of storytelling in leadership cannot be underestimated. Narratives allow people to connect on a human level, fostering empathy, understanding, and shared experiences. Emerging leaders often feel isolated in their struggles. When seasoned leaders open up about their missteps, hesitations, and moments of vulnerability, it creates an environment where honesty and growth flourish. This sharing of experiences makes leadership feel more attainable and less daunting for those who come after.

Consider the story of Maria, a CEO who rose through the ranks in a technology firm during a pivotal era of digital transformation. Her pathway to leadership was mired in challenges, including navigating gender biases and the daunting specter of self-doubt. As she climbed the corporate ladder, Maria vowed to maintain transparency and humility. She made it a priority to share her experiences candidly with her teams, whether they were discussing a failed project or the pressure of meeting aggressive deadlines.

Maria established mentorship programs within her organization, encouraging open dialogues where her younger colleagues could voice their uncertainties and learn from her mistakes. By candidly discussing her lessons learned, she championed a culture of vulnerability. During team meetings, she often emphasized how failure could be the stepping stone to innovation, urging her teams to view setbacks as valuable learning experiences rather than dead ends.

One memorable occasion resonated deeply with the young leaders who worked under her. During a company-wide meeting, Maria openly discussed a strategic decision she regretted—a project venture that failed to meet expectations. Instead of deflecting blame or sugarcoating the impact of her choices, she embraced her accountability. Employees shared later how this transparency transformed their perceptions of failure. It unshackled them from the paralyzing fear of making mistakes. The embrace of failure as part of the journey fostered courage, allowing for more creative solutions and innovations that ultimately benefited the company.

Leaders like Maria highlight a fundamental truth: vulnerability in leadership is not a weakness but a strength. By sharing her own story of growth, she encouraged younger leaders to embrace their authentic selves and laid the groundwork for a new leadership paradigm—one where human experiences are honored alongside corporate objectives.

Another inspiring leader, Damon, found himself in the spotlight during an economic downturn. As his organization struggled with dwindling revenue, he faced immense pressure to make significant cuts. However, rather than succumbing to a culture of fear and secrecy, Damon took a different approach. He assembled his leadership team, and together, they crafted a message of transparency about the organization's challenges. He emphasized that everyone had a role to play in navigating the crisis, fostering a spirit of collaboration across all levels of the company.

Damon's commitment to inclusion resonated deeply within his teams. By inviting input from employees and empowering them to contribute ideas for cost-saving measures, he cultivated a sense of ownership and shared purpose. This practice not only unveiled innovative solutions but also built resilience throughout the organization. Leaders who witnessed Damon's approach were inspired to adopt similar practices in their own spheres of influence. The willingness to create open channels of communication became a hallmark of his leadership style, ensuring that future leaders understood the value of collective problem-solving.

In sharing their experiences, leaders like Maria and Damon plant seeds of inspiration that can flourish among emerging leaders. But how do we ensure that these stories aren't just anecdotes but actionable insights for the future? It begins with deliberate guidance. Mentoring relationships are vital in this process. As leaders pass along lessons derived from tough calls and even tougher setbacks, they equip the next generation with tools to navigate complex, sometimes unforgiving landscapes.

Mentorship goes beyond formal programs; it involves nurturing relationships built on trust and mutual respect. By committing to regular interactions, established leaders can galvanize a new generation to proactively develop their leadership capabilities. They share not just hard-earned wisdom but actively listen and learn from the fresh perspectives of their mentees. This two-way exchange promotes a rich dialogue that can yield innovative ideas and inspire shared growth.

An inspiring example of mentorship in action comes from a global nonprofit organization where a veteran leader, Angela, has cultivated future leaders from diverse backgrounds. Angela has mentored countless individuals by sharing her global experiences navigating cultural complexities in leadership. More importantly, she emphasizes the importance of emotional intelligence in connecting with others. By modeling empathetic communication, Angela has empowered her mentees to embrace their unique backgrounds and incorporate their cultural insights into their leadership approaches.

This affirmation of individuality paves the way for a new era of leaders who are not only capable of strategic thinking but are also attuned to the nuances of human interaction. Angela's mentorship stories have become the evening sessions of reflection where young leaders gather to share their own experiences. So immersed are they in the storytelling tradition that many have stepped into their own roles as mentors, nurturing the next tier of leaders and perpetuating the cycle of inspiration.

Moreover, as we consider the attributes of effective leaders in today's world, there's an increasing focus on ethical leadership. In an age where transparency and accountability are paramount, leaders are tasked with not only achieving results but doing so with integrity. The transformational stories shared by experienced leaders play a significant role in instilling critical values such as honesty, fairness, and ethical responsibility among emerging leaders.

The journey of ethical leadership is encapsulated in the story of Samir, a leader in the financial sector who faced ethical dilemmas head-on. Samir's organization was thrust into a scandal involving unethical practices that came to light. Instead of shirking blame or attempting to placate stakeholders with hollow responses, he made a resolute decision to own the failures and rebuild the organization on the principles of integrity.

Samir articulated the lessons learned during this tumultuous time through workshops and discussions with both junior staff and upper management. His learning sessions became transformative opportunities, emphasizing the importance of ethical practices in every decision-making process—from everyday tasks to strategic planning.

Emerging leaders learned from Samir's transparency; they observed his commitment to ethical behavior in action and felt the weight of responsibility each time they made decisions. This example illustrated that embracing ethical leadership wasn't just about adhering to policies but involved a commitment to fostering a culture of integrity that considers every stakeholder's well-being.

Today's generation of leaders are more inclined to scrutinize the values that guide their actions in the workplace. They're less tolerant of the old paradigm that equated success with profit maximization at any cost. Instead, they champion sustainable practices, inclusivity, and social responsibility, challenging the status quo. By gleaning insights from established leaders like Samir who navigate ethical complexities, they reinforce the understanding that the long-term impact of their leadership choices extends far beyond quarterly results.

The process of inspiring future generations is a continuous and evolving journey. Just as the leaders before them have shared their lessons, younger leaders must recognize their role in this cycle. They, too, possess insights gained from contemporary challenges that can be valuable to peers and succeeding generations.

To promote this active exchange, emerging leaders should be encouraged to document their experiences and share learning moments within their networks and organizations. This advocacy for storytelling ensures that knowledge flows freely, creating a culture of shared responsibility in leadership development.

As organizations develop their leadership frameworks, they must prioritize platforms that facilitate storytelling and strengthen the bonds between current and future leaders. Creating spaces for dialogue—including workshops, leadership forums, and community-building initiatives—ensures that valuable insights from varying experiences are accessible and actionable. When leaders engage in these conversations, they cultivate an environment that values continuous learning, helping the next wave of leaders to stay true to their values while navigating their unique paths.

As we look to the horizon, it's clear that the influence of today's leaders resonates profoundly within the shaping of future generations. The stories shared—laced with wisdom, trials, and triumphs—become a gift that keeps on giving. Through these narratives, leaders equip younger generations with the tools to lead authentically, resolutely, and with an unwavering adherence to their values.

In this interconnected sphere of leadership, every interaction has the potential to inspire change. As Maria, Damon, Angela, and Samir have shown, great leaders don't merely look to leave behind a legacy of successes—they endeavor to ignite a passion for leadership that is grounded in humility, courage, and integrity.

Their stories serve as powerful reminders that leadership is a journey marked by learning and growth, a collaborative endeavor with no finish line. As emerging leaders take their place upon that continuum, they carry forward the torch, lighting the way for those who will follow, fostering a future where values and vision converge. Thus, the cycle of nurturing the next generation perpetuates, ensuring that the roots of principled leadership keep growing deeper as the branches extend ever wider.

CHAPTER TEN

Implementing the Balance

User-Friendly Strategy Development

As we conclude our exploration of the paradoxes of leadership, it is essential to consider how we implement the insights gathered into practical strategies that promote balance between tolerance and pride. The complexities of leadership do not yield simple solutions; however, creating user-friendly strategies can empower leaders to foster environments that encourage growth, accountability, and resilience. This subchapter will provide actionable steps to build a roadmap for integrating the principles of balance into your leadership practice.

To set the foundation, we will break down the process into three critical sections: establishing self-awareness through audits, creating effective team feedback loops, and implementing a cycle of continuous improvement. Each section will include methods, tools, and frameworks that can be tailored to meet the unique challenges of your organization.

Establishing Self-Awareness through Audits

Self-awareness is the cornerstone of effective leadership. It allows leaders to recognize their strengths and weaknesses, improving their capacity for empathy and adaptability. Self-audits serve as a diagnostic tool to help leaders gain insight into their behaviors, the organizational culture they cultivate, and how these factors affect team dynamics.

1. Conducting a Self-Audit

Begin with a comprehensive self-audit that reflects on your leadership style. This can be structured around three key questions:

- **What are my core leadership values?** Reflect on the principles that guide your decisions and interactions with your team. Are your values aligned with fostering both tolerance and pride?

- **Where do I exhibit excessive tolerance or pride?** Analyze instances where you may have overlooked critical feedback or avoided necessary confrontations. Conversely, consider moments when pride may have led to dismissal of valuable team insights.

- **How do others perceive my leadership?** Collect feedback from trusted colleagues or mentors who can provide an honest assessment of your leadership qualities. This feedback should focus on how your leaders exhibit pride and tolerance and their effects on team dynamics.

2. Tools for Self-Assessment

Utilize available resources and tools to support your self-audit:

- **360-Degree Feedback Surveys:** Involve team members at various levels to provide their perspectives on your leadership style. This comprehensive approach offers a well-rounded view of your influence on the organization.

- **Reflection Journals:** Maintain a journal to document your leadership journey. Regular entries can help you track your emotional responses, decision-making processes, and areas of improvement.

- **Personality Assessments:** Tools such as the Myers-Briggs Type Indicator or the DiSC profile can uncover your natural tendencies and areas for growth, informing strategies to balance your leadership presence.

Creating Effective Team Feedback Loops

Feedback is not just a tool for improvement; it is a vital component of a healthy organizational culture. Establishing mechanisms for team feedback promotes trust and accountability, encouraging open dialogue and collaboration.

1. Setting Up Structured Feedback Sessions

Organize regular feedback sessions that provide a safe space for dialogue. These sessions should prioritize open and honest communication:

- **Regular Check-ins:** Schedule bi-weekly or monthly check-ins where team members can express their thoughts on ongoing projects and collaborations. Ensure that this isn't a one-way street; make it clear that feedback is valuable at all levels.

- **Feedback Fridays:** Initiate a weekly opportunity for informal feedback sharing. Team members can come together to discuss accomplishments, challenges, and lessons learned in a relaxed setting.

- **Retrospectives:** After completing significant projects, hold retrospective meetings to analyze what worked, what didn't, and how the team can improve collectively. This formal reflection helps create a learning culture.

2. Encouraging Open-Ended Questions

Frame conversations around open-ended questions to stimulate deeper discussions:

- **What challenges did you face this past week, and how can we address them as a team?** This prompts problem-solving and clarifies the leader's position in facilitating growth.

- **How do you feel about the progress we are making toward our goals?** This encourages team members to reflect on their commitment and offers insights into group dynamics.

- **In what areas can I support you better?** This question opens the door to humility, inviting feedback about your leadership style and fostering trust.

3. Act on Feedback

Establish protocols for incorporating feedback into actionable plans. Key strategies include:

- **Documenting Feedback:** Ensure that feedback collected in sessions is documented collaboratively and shared with the entire team. This transparency reinforces the importance of contributions.

- **Creating Action Plans:** After collecting feedback, develop action plans with your team that address discussed areas for improvement. Assign responsibilities and follow up on progress regularly.

- **Recognizing Changes:** Celebrate successes tied to feedback implementation, reinforcing the importance of shared accountability and adjustments made from team input.

Implementing a Cycle of Continuous Improvement

The balance between tolerance and pride is not a one-time initiative; it requires ongoing effort. A culture of continuous improvement encourages adaptation and agility.

1. Establishing an Improvement Framework

Create a framework that guides your approach to continuous improvement:

- **Plan-Do-Check-Act (PDCA) Cycle:** This model encourages iterative learning. Plan for improvements, implement changes, observe the results, and act based on findings to refine processes further.

- **SMART Goals:** Set specific, measurable, achievable, relevant, and time-bound goals for both personal development and team milestones. Continuous check-ins on these goals keep the focus on progress rather than perfection.

- **Regular Training and Development:** Invest in training and professional development opportunities for both yourself and your team. Encourage learning environments where knowledge is shared rather than hoarded.

2. Building Resilience through Adaptability

To sustain a thriving atmosphere, leaders must shapeshift into resilient figures who embrace adaptability:

- **Promote a Growth Mindset:** Encourage team members to view challenges as opportunities for growth rather than setbacks. This mindset fosters a culture that welcomes constructive dissent and recognizes failures as stepping stones towards success.

- **Model Adaptability:** Demonstrate your willingness to learn and adapt in the face of change. Share personal stories of adjusting to feedback and changing circumstances to foster an environment where adaptability is normalized.

Conclusion: Actioning the Balance

Implementing user-friendly strategies for balance in leadership transforms the way you approach your team, fostering a culture of open communication and shared responsibility.

By establishing self-awareness, creating feedback loops, and committing to continuous improvement, leaders can cultivate an environment that thrives on resilience. Balancing tolerance and pride will not only enhance your leadership skills but also strengthen team dynamics, making for a more unified and innovative organization.

Strive for excellence while embracing the imperfections of the journey. The landscape of leadership is ever-changing, and by taking these actionable steps, you position yourself and your team to navigate it with agility and purpose. As you set forth on this journey, remember that every incremental effort counts toward building a robust leadership culture that future-proofs your organization in the face of challenges ahead.

Creating a Call to Action

As we come to the end of our exploration into the nuances of leadership—particularly the delicate interplay of pride and tolerance—it is essential to crystallize our insights into a resonant call to action. Leadership is not a static position; it is an evolving journey that demands both reflection and initiative. This journey rests not only on our understanding of leadership principles but, more importantly, on our commitment to translating those principles into tangible action.

To be effective leaders, we must recognize that every decision we make, every interaction we have, contributes to the broader narrative of our teams and organizations. Today's workplace is more dynamic than ever, influenced by rapid technological changes, shifting societal norms, and an increasingly diverse workforce. Within this context, the need for a balanced approach—one that harmonizes pride with humility and tolerance with accountability—is imperative.

Evolving our narratives about balance means more than just understanding the principles; it requires us to commit to actionable strategies that embody those principles daily. This commitment entails cultivating a mindset and habits that foster an environment where individuals feel empowered to voice their opinions, challenge the status quo, and actively engage in constructive conflict. As leaders, we must transform our insights into a clarion call—an urgent invitation to join us on this path of active engagement and continuous improvement.

Understanding the Importance of a Call to Action

The notion of a call to action often connotes a rallying cry, a moment of urgency that galvanizes individuals toward a common purpose. However, the essence of a successful call to action lies not just in its emotional appeal but in the clarity it offers. A compelling call to action should provide direction, instill a sense of urgency, and inspire commitment from every team member.

In the context of leadership, our call to action is twofold: it is about individual responsibility and collective accountability. Each leader must take a step back and ask themselves: *What does balance mean in my leadership practice? How am I actively promoting this balance within my team?* The answers to these questions can serve as a foundation for invoking a renewed commitment to effective leadership.

Consider the impactful leaders whose stories we've shared throughout this book. Each one faced challenges that tested their commitment to balance. Their journeys remind us that the path to effective leadership is fraught with complexity, requiring the courage to engage with uncomfortable truths about ourselves and our teams. In embracing this discomfort, we anchor our leadership in authenticity and resilience.

Fostering a Leadership Mindset

To evolve our narratives and translate them into our practices, we must first cultivate a leadership mindset that embraces growth, resilience, and adaptability. A mindset centered on continuous learning allows us to see challenges not as obstacles but as opportunities for development.

Creating a culture of balance begins with self-awareness. Leaders must engage in rigorous self-reflection, understanding their strengths and weaknesses as well as how their behaviors affect those around them. Rather than seeking perfect execution, we should aim for progress—celebrating small victories while remaining alert to areas that need improvement. We can ask ourselves:

- How do I react to feedback?

- Am I open to dissenting opinions?

- When was the last time I embraced vulnerability in my leadership?

The answers to these questions lay the groundwork for building a culture where all voices are valued, and every team member feels an integral part of the leadership journey.

Communicating the Vision

As leaders, we have the duty to communicate our vision effectively. Our call to action must be grounded in a clear articulation of our objectives and the collective journey ahead. We must ensure that our teams understand not only what is expected of them but why those expectations matter.

Articulating a compelling vision involves framing it in a way that resonates personally with each team member. Leaders should take the time to share personal stories that connect their values with the organizational goals. Engaging in transparent dialogue allows employees to see beyond their daily tasks and understand how their contributions fit into the larger picture.

This process not only fosters a sense of accountability but also empowers individuals to become advocates for the culture of balance we seek to instill. When employees can store the vision in their own narratives, their investment in the attainability of those goals deepens.

Promoting a Culture of Experimentation

With this call to action firmly established, the next step is to promote a culture that welcomes experimentation and embraces failure as part of the learning process. Encouraging innovation means recognizing that there is inherent value in taking risks, trying new approaches, and even stumbling along the way.

One of the most critical aspects of this cultural shift lies in creating safe spaces where team members can voice their thoughts and concerns without fear of reprisal. Constructive conflict should not be seen as a threat; rather, it can be viewed as an opportunity to refine ideas and approach challenges from multiple perspectives. This openness propels us forward, allowing us to harness diversity of thought as a catalyst for innovation.

As leaders, we can foster this climate of experimentation by actively rewarding creative problem-solving, prioritizing collaboration, and sharing lessons learned from both successes and failures. The more we celebrate process over perfection, the more likely our teams will feel encouraged to take initiative.

Setting Measurable Goals

To translate our vision and call to action into reality, we must set clear, measurable goals that drive accountability. These objectives should align with the principles of balance, serving as benchmarks for both individual and team performance.

SMART goals—specific, measurable, achievable, relevant, and time-bound—serve as effective markers in this endeavor. By establishing actionable goals, we lend ourselves a framework within which to operate, evaluate progress, and recalibrate when necessary. It is vital that leaders communicate these objectives regularly, offering opportunities for feedback and reflection along the journey.

Development plans should be flexible and adaptable, catering to the unique dynamics of each team. Emphasizing regular check-ins ensures that we remain aligned with our goals while remaining receptive to feedback. This iterative approach positions us to learn organically from both successes and setbacks, reinforcing a culture of growth.

Empowering Others to Lead

Creating a ripple effect of balance across an organization requires us to empower others to take ownership of their leadership journeys. As leaders, we must act as facilitators, guiding team members to find their voices and strengths.

Encouragement plays a crucial role in this empowerment. Leaders should provide opportunities for individuals to lead initiatives, voice ideas, and make decisions that affect their work. This not only builds confidence but also fosters a sense of agency among team members.

In parallel, we should instill mentorship programs that facilitate knowledge sharing and personal development. By investing in the growth of our emerging leaders, we cultivate a leadership pipeline that is diverse, dynamic, and equipped to tackle the challenges ahead.

Modeling the Behavior We Seek

As leaders, we must continuously model the behavior we expect from our teams. This includes demonstrating vulnerability, embracing feedback, and owning our mistakes. Acknowledging when we falter not only reinforces our authenticity but also encourages the same openness in others.

When leaders allow themselves to be human, they create an environment where it is normal to be imperfect yet resilient. By prioritizing humility, we break down barriers that might hinder collaboration, fostering deeper connections within our teams.

Additionally, practicing gratitude and recognition deepens the bonds within our teams. Acknowledging the contributions of others reinforces their value and bridges the gap between hierarchy and teamwork. Celebrating the small achievements creates a community ethos where everyone feels they play an integral role in the organization's success.

Taking Ownership of the Collective Future

Finally, a successful call to action must be rooted in collective ownership. Leaders need to instill a sense of purpose that resonates through every level of the organization. Encourage your team to envision what success looks like and actively engage them in shaping that future.

Each team member should feel a part of the narrative, contributing their perspectives toward a shared mission. Facilitate conversations that allow individuals to express concerns, aspirations, and ideas freely. This ensures that everyone has a voice in the direction we take, fostering a sense of ownership, loyalty, and dedication to our goals.

As we embark on this journey of implementing balance in our leadership, let us remember that the call to action isn't merely a moment; it is a commitment to a process. It is about the choices we make, the attitudes we adopt, and the influence we wield.

A Note on Courage

Embracing this journey will certainly demand courage. It will require us to face uncomfortable truths and dismantle long-standing habits that no longer serve us or our teams. As we stand at the precipice of this evolving narrative, let courage guide us—not just in our leadership roles but in every interaction we have with those around us.

Active participation in this process of change invites everyone—leaders, teams, and individuals alike—to rise to the occasion. We harness our collective strength to create a landscape where innovation and accountability coexist, birthing a new era of leadership that is both empowering and resilient.

In conclusion, as you leave this chapter, allow the spirit of inquiry to seep into the fabric of your daily leadership practices. Let balance be your guiding light as you evolve your narrative, embracing the full spectrum of what it means to lead with integrity, purpose, and humility. Together, we can create a future that not only honors individual contributions but also honors our shared commitment to progress and excellence. The mantle of leadership is heavy, but within it lies the unparalleled opportunity to inspire change. Let us seize that opportunity with fervor.

Reflecting on the Journey

Throughout this book, we have navigated the intricate landscapes of leadership, encountering the nuances of tolerance and pride along the way. As we arrive at this final segment, it becomes imperative to pause and reflect on the understanding we have cultivated. Every leader's journey is unique, yet the essence of leadership binds us together in shared experiences. Together, we have unveiled the paradoxes of these virtues, shedding light on how they can uplift or undermine our effectiveness as leaders.

In essence, leadership is a journey—a continuous odyssey filled with winding paths, unexpected turns, and profound discoveries. It is more than merely holding a position of authority; it encompasses the responsibility of guiding others while remaining open to personal evolution and growth. This subchapter invites you to reflect on your own leadership journey and the lessons woven through it, urging you to embrace self-communication and introspection.

A journey worth taking begins with reflection. Looking back at our earlier discussions, we explored the idealization of leadership and the unrealistic expectations placed upon those in leadership positions. Recall the stories of leaders who grappled with the burden of perfectionism, facing burnout in their pursuit of an unattainable ideal. These narratives serve as an invitation to recognize our imperfections, not as shortcomings but as essential facets of our humanity.

As you reflect on your own journey, consider the moments when your desire for success cultivated an unhealthy obsession with perfection. Have you ever felt that the weight of expectations caused you to lose sight of your core values? In moments of self-discovery, it is crucial to acknowledge the lessons learned from past missteps. Embracing our flaws fosters growth, paving the way for a healthier and more resilient leadership approach. By acknowledging our own vulnerabilities, we cultivate empathy and authenticity that resonate with our teams.

Our exploration of tolerance revealed both its strength and its propensity to breed complacency. It is essential to ask ourselves: in our pursuit of harmony, have we tolerated dissenting voices or avoided necessary conversations? As leaders, we often find ourselves standing at a crossroads, tempted to choose the path of ease over engagement. Taking an honest inventory of your actions can illuminate opportunities for growth. Reflect on instances where you may have sidestepped discomfort in favor of a harmonious facade.

The fog of tolerance can obscure our vision, leading us to overlook the discontent simmering beneath the surface. Use this opportunity to engage in self-communication, sharing your insights with your trusted mentors or peers. Discuss your experiences candidly and seek their perspectives to enhance your understanding. The act of verbalizing your thoughts can solidify insights and facilitate deeper comprehension of your leadership style.

As we delved into the relationship between pride and arrogance, the importance of humility emerged as a key theme. Ask yourself whether pride has ever veered into arrogance in your leadership journey. Have you, at times, been dismissive of valuable feedback, blinded by your own achievements? It is crucial to recognize that the most successful leaders are those who embody humility and are receptive to critique. Reflect on your willingness to accept feedback and admit misjudgments. When was the last time you sought input from your team or acknowledged a mistake in front of them? It's in those seemingly small acts of vulnerability that we exercise true leadership.

Exploring the effects of complacency highlighted the significance of constant reflection as a counterbalance. In what ways have you remained steadfast in your comfort zones? Consider those missed opportunities for innovation and growth brought about by complacency. Reflect on moments where you recognized the need for change but hesitated to act. How did that impact your organization and the morale of your team? Commitment to introspection requires confronting our inertia and face the subsequent ripple effects throughout our organizations.

As leaders reflecting on our collective journeys, it becomes increasingly evident that vulnerability is not a liability but a powerful strength. Sharing our growth journeys and personal challenges humanizes the leadership experience and builds stronger bonds within our teams. Recall the stories of leaders who embraced their weaknesses; they fostered an environment where others felt safe to express their own struggles. What steps can you take to share your experiences and encourage openness among your team members? Let the warmth of your vulnerability guide them in fostering their growth.

After all, true leadership is not about positioning oneself above others; it's about walking alongside your team on a shared journey of discovery and achievement. Each decision strengthens or weakens the fabric of trust within your organization. Reflect on how you can nurture an environment where pride and humility coexist, where team members can confidently express their thoughts while feeling respected and valued.

As we explore the path to sustainable change, it becomes clear that each leader has a responsibility to continuously cultivate a culture of adaptability and resilience. Take a moment to assess your organization's readiness for change. Are there behaviors or mindsets that have hindered your ability to pivot and respond to fluctuations in the industry? Remember, as leaders, we are always encouraged to lead by example.

Infusing practices of humility, continual learning, and open communication can transform rigid structures into agile teams. Reflect on strategies you can implement to foster these practices. Consider establishing regular check-in meetings that focus on learning rather than performance metrics. This space should be designated for open dialogue and reflection, where team members can share insights, lessons learned, and constructive critiques. Positioning these conversations as opportunities for growth instead of faultfinding reinforces your commitment to transparent and constructive communication.

The stories of leaders we have shared throughout this book embody the embodiment of resilience and adaptability. Take time to draw strength from their experiences as you reflect on your path ahead. What legacies do you wish to create? Which qualities do you aspire to instill within your organization? Recognizing the impact of your leadership style not only shapes your journey but also sets the precedent for future leaders who will follow in your footsteps.

In conclusion, as you reflect on your journey, remember that leadership is a continuous process of self-discovery and evolution. Embrace your imperfections, nurture your relationships with pride and humility, and open yourself to the transformative power of vulnerability. Your leadership choices will ripple through your teams and organizations, influencing their culture and shaping their growth.

The ultimate takeaway lies in your willingness to communicate openly with yourself and your teams. Encourage dialogue around these pivotal themes, allowing space for exploration and introspection. As leaders, your reflections are not final; they are the beginning of deeper conversations that can lead to newfound growth.

Let us step forward, filled with pride in our progress but grounded in the humility to learn from our experiences and the experiences of those around us. This journey is not a solitary endeavor; it is shared among the leaders of today and tomorrow. Nurture these relationships and continue the discourse, guiding one another through the labyrinth of leadership.

As we close this chapter, remember that the essence of effective leadership lies in our ability to balance pride and humility, transcending the paradoxes that often challenge us. Embrace the journey, cherish the lessons, and let them guide your path ahead into the landscape of possibility and change.

Until We Meet Again

As we wrap up this journey through 'Enigma in the Shadows,' I just want to take a moment to express my deepest gratitude to you for coming along for the ride! Your choice to dive into this realm means the world to me, and I hope you found the adventure as exhilarating as I did. Each character's journey was crafted with care, and I genuinely hope they resonated with you in some way. Thank you for allowing these tales to intertwine with your thoughts and emotions. It's been an incredible experience to share this narrative with you, exploring the depths of mystery and the intricacies of the human spirit. You've journeyed through the highs, the lows, and the unexpected twists—just as life often does. It encouraged me to rethink and reflect long after typing the final word, and I hope you experienced that too. As we conclude, remember that the stories don't end here; they continue to live on in your mind and heart. I encourage you to carry these characters and their journeys with you, as they are now intertwined with your own experiences. Reflect on the themes that emerged, the questions that linger, and allow them to inspire your own life's adventures. If any part of this book sparked a fire within you, I'd love to hear your thoughts. Let's connect! Share your insights, feelings, or even that "ah-ha!" moment you had. I would adore keeping this conversation alive, and who knows, maybe there will be more stories in the future that we can navigate together. Your presence as a reader gives meaning to this work, and I cannot thank you enough. May the exhilaration of this journey prompt you to seek your mystery, embrace every shadow, and step boldly into the light. Keep those eyes open and your heart racing because the world is full of enigmas waiting to be unraveled. Until we meet again, may your adventures be thrilling and your stories be profoundly yours. Keep reading, dreaming, and discovering!

With heartfelt thanks
Digvijay Mourya